Everything I Know I Learned from Disney Animated Feature Films

Everything I Know I Learned from Disney Animated Feature Films

Advice for Living Happily Ever After

Jim Korkis

Author of THE VAULT OF WALT series

Theme Park Press
www.ThemeParkPress.com

© 2015 Jim Korkis

No part of this publication may be reproduced, distributed, or transmitted in any form or by any means, including photocopying, recording, or other electronic or mechanical methods, without the prior written permission of the publisher, except for brief quotations embodied in critical reviews and certain other noncommercial uses permitted by copyright law.

Although every precaution has been taken to verify the accuracy of the information contained herein, no responsibility is assumed for any errors or omissions, and no liability is assumed for damages that may result from the use of this information.

Theme Park Press is not associated with the Walt Disney Company.

The views expressed in this book are those of the author and do not necessarily reflect the views of Theme Park Press.

Theme Park Press publishes its books in a variety of print and electronic formats. Some content that appears in one format may not appear in another.

Editor: Bob McLain
Layout: Artisanal Text

ISBN 978-1-941500-52-1
Printed in the United States of America

Theme Park Press | www.ThemeParkPress.com
Address queries to bob@themeparkpress.com

This book is dedicated to Owen Suskind who has shown the world that the magic behind the words in Disney Animated Feature Films can heal, inspire, and even break the bonds of autism. His story is shared in the book Life, Animated: A Story of Sidekicks, Heroes and Autism *(Kingswell, 2014) written by his father Ron Suskind.*

Contents

Introduction	xi
Snow White and the Seven Dwarfs (1937)	1
Pinocchio (1940)	4
Fantasia (1940)	7
Dumbo (1941)	10
Bambi (1942)	13
Saludos Amigos (1943)	16
The Three Caballeros (1945)	19
Make Mine Music (1946)	22
Fun and Fancy Free (1947)	25
Melody Time (1948)	28
The Adventures of Ichabod and Mr. Toad (1949)	31
Cinderella (1950)	34
Alice in Wonderland (1951)	37
Peter Pan (1953)	40
Lady and the Tramp (1955)	43
Sleeping Beauty (1959)	46
101 Dalmations (1961)	49
The Sword in the Stone (1963)	52
The Jungle Book (1967)	55
The Aristocats (1970)	58
Robin Hood (1973)	61

The Many Adventures of Winnie the Pooh (1977)	64
The Rescuers (1977)	67
The Fox and the Hound (1981)	70
The Black Cauldron (1985)	73
The Great Mouse Detective (1986)	76
Oliver & Company (1988)	79
The Little Mermaid (1989)	82
The Rescuers Down Under (1990)	85
Beauty and the Beast (1991)	88
Aladdin (1992)	91
The Lion King (1994)	94
Pocahontas (1995)	97
The Hunchback of Notre Dame (1996)	100
Hercules (1997)	103
Mulan (1998)	106
Tarzan (1999)	109
Fantasia 2000 (1999)	112
Dinosaur (2000)	115
The Emperor's New Groove (2000)	118
Atlantis: The Lost Empire (2001)	121
Lilo and Stitch (2002)	124
Treasure Planet (2002)	127
Brother Bear (2003)	130
Home on the Range (2004)	133
Chicken Little (2005)	136
Meet the Robinsons (2007)	139
Bolt (2008)	142

The Princess and the Frog (2009)	145
Tangled (2010)	148
Winnie the Pooh (2011)	151
Wreck-It Ralph (2012)	154
Frozen (2013)	157
Big Hero 6 (2014)	160
About the Author	163
More Books from Theme Park Press	165

Introduction

Walt Disney's *Snow White and the Seven Dwarfs* (1937) was the first U.S. animated feature film. It was also the first animated feature to be produced using cel animation and made in color.

As early as 1932, Walt Disney considered making a feature-length animated film. In May 1933, it was announced that Walt was developing Lewis Carroll's *Alice in Wonderland*. Popular silent screen actress Mary Pickford would appear as a live-action Alice in an animated wonderland. When Paramount Pictures released their fully live-action version of the Carroll story in December 1933, however, it killed the Disney project.

Walt then initiated talks with his friend and folk comedian Will Rogers to star in a feature-length film entitled *Rip Van Winkle*. Rogers would have appeared as the title character in live action, but the world with the little bearded men playing at nine pins would have been animated. Rogers' untimely death in a plane crash brought an end to that film.

Around the same time, Walt was also in discussions with *King Kong* film producer Merian C. Cooper about a co-production to make an animated feature of Victor Herbert's operetta *Babes in Toyland*. Cooper worked at RKO, which owned the rights.

No one had ever made a traditional feature-length cartoon because it was assumed audiences wouldn't sit still long enough and would quickly become bored with joke after joke. Others proclaimed that the bright cartoon colors would irritate eyes watching for that amount of time. Adults, it was felt, wouldn't pay to see a fairy tale.

"You should have heard the howls of warning when we started making a full-length cartoon," said Walt. "It was prophesied that nobody would sit through such a thing. But there was only one way we could do it successfully and that was to plunge ahead and go for broke—shoot the works. There could be no compromising on money, talent, or time."

In 1933, Willard G. Triest, working in Sweden for the vice president of United Artists film distribution, put together a fifty-five minute compilation of Disney short cartoons to promote those cartoons in Scandinavia. It was an immediate sell-out in theaters in Sweden, prompting additional prints to be made for theaters in Norway and Denmark, and followed by similar long running releases of this program in twenty other countries, including France.

The continued success of the cartoon compilation, drawing big audiences waiting in lines outside the theaters to see the show, convinced Walt that American audiences would accept a feature length animated film.

By October 1934, Walt had made his decision that his first animated feature film would be based on the story of Snow White. The story was not so much inspired by the original Brothers Grimm fairy tale as by the 1916 silent film adaptation that Walt had seen as a teenager.

"I once saw Marguerite Clark performing in it in Kansas City when I was a newsboy. It was one of the first big feature pictures I'd ever seen. I thought it was the perfect story. It had the sympathetic dwarfs, you see? It had the heavy. It had the prince and the girl. The romance. I just thought it was a perfect story," recalled Walt.

While in production, *Snow White and the Seven Dwarfs* was ridiculed by Hollywood as "Disney's Folly".

When the film premiered at the Carthay Circle Theater in Hollywood in December 1937, it sent shockwaves through the film industry because it was just as good if not better than the best of Hollywood's live-action films.

In fact, it became the highest grossing film of all time, and was only dethroned from that position by the release of *Gone with the Wind* in 1939.

The success of *Snow White* prompted other film studios to put into production such fantasy films as MGM's *The Wizard of Oz* and Max Fleischer's *Gulliver's Travels*.

Walt, in anticipation of the success of his film, had already acquired a multitude of other properties and had them in various stages of development.

This was the beginning of Walt Disney Feature Animation that became for decades the pre-eminent animation studio. Its development of technology and production processes, along with its quality approach to content and personality animation, influenced other animation studios worldwide.

With Walt's death in 1966, the Disney Company continued to make significant animated feature films. In 1989, with the release of *The Little Mermaid*, the studio once again "re-invented" the format and had a string of hugely popular feature films including ones produced at two annex studios: *Mulan* (1998) and *Lilo and Stitch* (2002) from Walt Disney Feature Animation Florida (1989–2004) and *Tarzan* (1999) from Walt Disney Feature Animation France (1994–2003). One of the most recent Walt Disney Feature Animation films, *Frozen* (2013), is the highest grossing animated feature film ever produced, winning Academy Awards for Best Animated Feature Film and Best Original Song.

Zootopia, Disney's 55th animated feature film, is scheduled for release on March 4, 2016, and *Moana*, its 56th film, for November 23, 2016.

The Story Behind the Quotes

For decades, the animated feature films produced by the Disney Company have entertained and inspired. They contain many memorable phrases that are sometimes paraphrased or misquoted. For example, many believe that the evil queen in *Snow White and the Seven Dwarfs* (1937) said, "Mirror, Mirror on the wall" when she actually intoned "Magic Mirror on the wall".

My goal was to capture the actual words from each film and, when possible, to avoid the more familiar phrases like "Some day my prince will come" or "Let it go", and to spotlight instead some often forgotten gems.

Accordingly, this book contains four quotes from each of the official fifty-four animated feature films produced by Walt Disney Feature Animation from 1937–2014. It does not contain quotes from the:

- Feature films produced by Walt Disney Productions that were primarily live action, but featured significant segments of animation, like *Song of the South* (1946), *So Dear to My Heart* (1948), *Mary Poppins* (1964), and *Pete's Dragon* (1977).

- Forty-six animated features from DisneyToon Studios, even though some of these films received a theatrical release, including *A Goofy Movie* (1995), *Return to Neverland* (2002), *Piglet's Big Movie* (2003), and *Planes* (2013).

- Fifteen animated features produced by Pixar. Even though The Walt Disney Company purchased Pixar in 2006, it is operated as a separate entity from Walt Disney Feature Animation.

- Stop-motion animated films produced by The Walt Disney Company, including *The Nightmare Before Christmas* (1993) and *James and the Giant Peach* (1996).

- The animated features that The Walt Disney Company has acquired over the years, or ones that it merely distributes, like the Hayao Miyazaki films made for Studio Ghibli.

Inside this book are not always the most familiar or common of quotes, but ones that were selected to make readers think about the philosophy and quality of life.

During Walt Disney's lifetime, the dialog in a Disney animated feature was contributed by a variety of writers (some only supplying one or two lines), including Walt himself. For instance, it was Walt who came up with the phrase "Zip-A-Dee-Doo-Dah Day".

However, Walt had to approve every word that was in a Disney animated feature film during his lifetime and it had to reflect his thoughts and feelings.

A full script was not written out, unlike it is for live-action films, because animation is primarily a visual medium and action, rather than dialog, was strongly emphasized.

"Walt usually left off the dialogue until a sequence had been developed to the point where he could see just how little was really needed," wrote Frank Thomas and Ollie Johnston. "The storyman had to think in visual terms first, and when he did write dialogue, it had to tell something about the character and not be exposition. Walt insisted that no one wants to see a character chewing on a bunch of words when a provocative situation is developing."

Selecting significant quotations from these films was sometimes challenging because they feature fewer words than a regular live-action film. For instance, *Bambi* (1942) contains roughly 950 spoken words in the entire film.

"Dialogue was kept to a minimum. We are striving for fewer words because we wanted the action and the music to carry it," recalled Walt.

(Ironically, the longest quotation in this book comes from *Bambi*.)

Often, the song lyrics conveyed the thoughts of the characters quicker and more effectively than dialog, just like in a Broadway theater production. Princess Aurora in *Sleeping Beauty* (1959) only has eighteen lines of dialogue. Her thoughts and feelings are communicated through her songs.

Legendary Disney storyman Bill Peet was the first person to ever write an entire Disney animated feature by himself. That film was *101 Dalmatians* (1961) and it became the tenth highest grossing film of the year and one of the studio's most popular films.

The author of the original book, Dodie Smith, sent Peet a letter saying that Peet actually improved her story and his designs looked better than the illustrations in her book.

Peet continued to work on the next Disney animated features, but left the company during the story development for *The Jungle Book* (1967) because of continuing disagreements with Walt. Peet went on to a highly successful career as a children's book writer and illustrator.

Linda Woolverton was the first woman to write a Disney animated feature film, *Beauty and the Beast* (1991). She wrote the story draft before storyboarding began and then worked closely with the animators to continue developing the story. She also co-wrote the story for *The Lion King* (1994).

When Michael Eisner joined the company as CEO in 1984, he openly admitted he had difficulty following the story and the character arcs on storyboards. He claimed that when the animators were showing him one board and explaining the action, he could never quite remember clearly what was on an earlier storyboard.

"If we're going to produce new classics," Eisner told co-directors Ron Clement and John Musker when they pitched him the storyboard for *The Great Mouse Detective*, "then we have to begin with a script, just the way we do with the rest of our movies."

Since Eisner's background was in live-action films at Paramount like *Raiders of the Lost Ark* and *Beverly Hills Cop*, he had no clue how radical that suggestion was for a Disney animated feature. For fifty years, stories for animated features were always done on a series of four-by-eight storyboards.

Disney artist Webb Smith (who wanted to be a comic strip artist) is credited with creating the basic concept. He was tacking with push pins little thumbnail drawings to the wall of his office to get a sense of the flow of a scene. Walt worried about damage to the wall with all those tiny holes and wanted something less confined to just one particular location.

A storyboard is a cork board about four feet high by eight feet long. Story sketches with the dialog written underneath were put in sequence on these boards with pushpins so they could be easily added, removed, or rearranged in the process of developing a story. It was almost like a giant, ever-changing comic strip.

Disney was the first animation studio to utilize storyboards for animation and one of the first studios to utilize storyboards for an entire film, *20,000 Leagues Under the Sea* (1954). It was so effective that the use of storyboards became standard practice not only in animation but live action.

Some live-action film directors like Alfred Hitchcock had used storyboards to plan out a particular sequence. MGM did it for the burning of Atlanta in *Gone with the Wind* (1939) because it could only be filmed once.

A storyboard can hold up to 100 drawings. For Pixar's first animated feature, *Toy Story* (1995), over 25,000 boards were used.

The shift to having a full script first helped spark the renaissance in Disney animation beginning in the 1990s by producing stronger stories that had resolved many challenges before being storyboarded. However, some things could only be resolved once they were on the storyboard.

In *Beauty and the Beast* (1991), the items in the Beast's kitchen sing the tune "Be Our Guest" to Maurice, Belle's father, because he is the first visitor to the castle in years. Once it was on the storyboards, it was clear that the story was about the relationship of Belle and the Beast, not Maurice, so all the storyboard drawings of Maurice were torn up and replaced with new drawings of Belle, while the rest of the drawings remained the same.

Many Disney animated feature films were overflowing with so many wonderful words of wisdom that it was a challenge to just select only four examples from each film. With other films it was more of a challenge to find four phrases at the same level that could stand alone and not need additional explanation.

As I mentioned, I wanted to spotlight some of the words of insight that most of us have forgotten, but were significant in the films in terms of giving advice on how to behave and live your life.

I had the pleasurable, but time-consuming experience of sitting down and watching all the films again in order to get the correct wording, to rediscover new gems of wisdom, and to be engulfed in a world where it was entirely reasonable that people could live happily ever after.

To help set these quotes in context, I have included a brief summary of the film to spark some memories and have included some behind-the-scenes information as well.

Hopefully, the quotes that were finally selected may stir the desire for readers to go back and rediscover some of these films and to reconsider what is truly important in life.

Jim Korkis
Disney Historian
July 2015

Snow White and the Seven Dwarfs (1937)

Based on the Grimm's fairy tale, a happy and beautiful young princess named Snow White is almost killed by her wicked and vain stepmother, the Queen, when the Magic Mirror reveals that Snow White is the fairest in the land. Saved at the last moment by a sympathetic huntsman, Snow White runs deep into the forest where she stumbles upon the cottage of seven dwarfs: Doc, Grumpy, Sleepy, Happy, Bashful, Sneezy, and Dopey. They vow to protect her and, in return, she takes care of them and the cottage.

The Queen discovers that Snow White still lives and uses black magic to disguise herself as an old hag peddler woman. In addition, she conjures up a poisoned apple and tricks Snow White into taking a bite when the dwarfs are away at their diamond mine. The girl falls into a deathlike state. Warned by the forest animals, the dwarfs rush back to the cottage and, after a dramatic chase, the Queen dies.

Believing the girl to be dead, they build an aboveground glass coffin where she is discovered by the Prince who is able to revive her with true love's first kiss and they live happily ever after.

Behind the Animation

- A special Academy Award for the film consisting of a regular Oscar statuette and seven smaller sized ones was presented to Walt Disney in 1939 by ten-year old actress Shirley Temple. It is now at the Walt Disney Family Museum in San Francisco.

- *Snow White* was the first animated feature to be selected for the National Film Registry. Established in 1988, the NFR acknowledges a few culturally, historically, or aesthetically significant films each year. Other Disney films in the NFR are *Fantasia* (1940), *Bambi* (1942), *Beauty and the Beast* (1989), and *Mary Poppins* (1964).

- In 1939, the Nazi Propaganda Ministry purchased 50 American films, but they were never shown in Germany at that time due to growing anti-Americanism. Adolf Hitler had a copy of *Snow White* delivered to his private movie theater in Ubersalzberg and considered it one of the greatest movies ever made.

- Disney had initially budgeted the film between $150,000 and $250,000, but the final cost came to over $1.5 million.

- Some of the fifty names considered for the dwarfs, but rejected, include: Snoopy, Crabby, Gloomy, Dizzy, Daffy, Blabby, Jumpy, Goopy, Hotsy, and Snappy.

Quotable Quotes

She's a female! And all females is poison! They're full of wicked wiles!

— Grumpy

....

When there's too much to do, don't let it bother you. Forget your troubles and whistle while you work.

— Snow White

....

With a smile and a song, life is just like a bright sunny day. Your cares fade away and your heart is young.

— Snow White

....

You don't know what I've been through and all because I was afraid.

— Snow White

Pinocchio (1940)

The film tells the story of an old and lonely woodcarver named Gepetto and the wooden boy marionette he makes out of pine named Pinocchio. At night, the Blue Fairy grants the old man's wish for the puppet to come to life. To become a real boy, Pinocchio must prove himself to be brave, truthful, and unselfish.

The Blue Fairy appoints little Jiminy Cricket to act as the boy's conscience and to help him choose between right and wrong. The next morning, on his way to the first day of school, Pinocchio is led astray by the unscrupulous fox Honest John and his companion, Gideon the mute cat, and finds himself trapped into performing for the evil puppeteer Stromboli.

The Blue Fairy frees Pinocchio from his enslavement, but the puppet is once again tricked by Honest John and his mute sidekick, and is taken to Pleasure Island where bad boys who make bad decisions are transformed into donkeys.

Escaping just in time, Pinocchio and Jiminy find that Gepetto has been lost at sea trying to find his missing boy. In a dramatic finale, the pair rescues the toymaker from Monstro the whale and Pinocchio's brave act transforms him into a real boy.

Behind the Animation

- It was Walt Disney who felt Jiminy Cricket should stay alive so Pinocchio had someone to talk to during his adventures and dubbed him "Jiminy" after a popular expression of the time. In the original novel, Pinocchio kills the talking cricket.

- Evelyn Venable who did the live-action reference modeling and voice for the Blue Fairy was also the model for the original Torch Lady logo used by Columbia Pictures at the beginning of all its films.

- *Pinocchio* was the first Disney animated feature to win an Oscar in a competitive category for Best Song: "When You Wish Upon A Star".

- When the film was released, Paolo Lorenzini, the nephew of Carlo Lorenzini (who under the name "Collodi" wrote the original book), begged the Italian Ministry of Popular Culture to sue Walt Disney for libel in portraying Pinocchio "so he easily could be mistaken for an American" instead of an Italian.

- The Pinocchio puppet built for use as an animation model was lost for fifty years until it was discovered stuffed in a forgotten cabinet at the studio when the phone company came to remove some old wires.

Quotable Quotes

A lie keeps growing and growing until it's as plain as the nose on your face.
— The Blue Fairy

Always let your conscience be your guide.
— The Blue Fairy

A conscience is that still small voice that people won't listen to. That's just the trouble with the world today.
— Jiminy Cricket

When you wish upon a star, makes no difference who you are, anything your heart desires will come to you.
— Jiminy Cricket

Fantasia (1940)

Fantasia was originally titled *The Concert Feature* and is a compilation of various independent animated segments interpreting classical music with no central protagonist or dialog connecting them.

The compositions include Johann Sebastian Bach's "Toccata and Fugue in D Minor" using abstract imagery; Pyotr Ilyich Tchaikovsky's "The Nutcracker Suite" with ethereal fairies and Hop Low and his fellow mushroom dancers; Paul Dukas' "The Sorcerer's Apprentice" starring Mickey Mouse as an apprentice to the sorcerer Yen Sid and famously abusing his magic; and Igor Stravinsky's "The Rite of Spring" set to the evolution of the world with images of the reign of the mighty dinosaurs

The film also features Ludwig van Beethoven's "The Pastoral Symphony" using Mount Olympus and characters from Greek myths in a playful picnic; Amilcare Ponchielli's "Dance of the Hours" as performed by balletic dancing alligators, ostriches, elephants, and hippos; and Modest Mussorgsky's "Night on Bald Mountain" with the theme of evil demons led by the overwhelming Chernabog who are overcome by the sound of religious pilgrims singing Franz Schubert's "Ave Maria" as church bells ring and dawn returns.

Each of these pieces was conducted by the legendary Leopold Stokowski with the Philadelphia Orchestra and is hosted by noted music critic and historian Deems Taylor.

Behind the Animation

- The sorcerer named Yen Sid ("Disney" spelled backwards) who distinctively raises just one eyebrow when annoyed was modeled after Walt Disney. The first time that Yen Sid ever spoke was in a 1971 episode of *The Wonderful World of Disney* called "Disney on Parade", voiced by the late Michael Rye.

- At 125 minutes in length, *Fantasia* is the longest Disney animated feature ever made. The shortest is *Saludos Amigos* (1943) at 42 minutes.

- It was Walt Disney's intention to keep the film in continual release by replacing existing segments with new episodes interpreting other classical music selections. Story material was developed for additional pieces including "Ride of the Valkyries" by Richard Wagner, "The Swan of Tuonela" by Jean Sibelius, "Invitation to the Dance" by Carl Maria von Weber, "Flight of the Bumblebee" by Nikolai Rimsky-Korsakov, and others.

- "Ave Maria" is the only musical selection in the film to feature vocals. All other selections are strictly instrumental.

- As the first feature film shown in four track stereophonic sound, *Fantasia* was recorded in a process known as Fantasound, invented specifically for this soundtrack and developed by RCA and William E. Garity of Walt Disney Productions.

Quotable Quotes

The one composition of Tchaikovsky's that he really detested was his "Nutcracker Suite", which is probably the most popular thing he ever wrote.

— Deems Taylor

....

A legend about a sorcerer who had an apprentice. He was a bright young lad; very anxious to learn the business. As a matter of fact, he was a little bit too bright, because he started practicing some of the boss' best magic tricks before learning how to control them.

— Deems Taylor

....

We hear the "Ave Maria" with its message of the triumph of hope and life over the powers of despair and death.

— Deems Taylor

....

What you're going to see are the designs and pictures and stories that music inspired in the minds and imaginations of a group of artists. In other words, these are not going to be the interpretations of trained musicians, which I think is all to the good.

— Deems Taylor

Dumbo (1941)

Storks deliver new babies to the animals in a circus train in Florida, including baby elephant Jumbo Jr. to his mother. Because of his overly large ears, he is cruelly nicknamed "Dumbo" by others.

As a result of protecting her son from physical abuse from some teenagers at the circus, Mrs. Jumbo is locked away in a small circus wagon as a "mad elephant".

Dumbo's ears trip him up during a spectacular elephant pyramid stunt and he is shunned by the other elephants. He is relegated to being a part of a demeaning clown act featuring firemen rescuing the elephant baby.

Dumbo's only friend is Timothy Mouse, another outcast, who constantly encourages Dumbo. After drinking from a tub of water that has been polluted by a bottle of champagne, Dumbo and Timothy fantasize about pink elephants on parade and awake to find themselves high in a tree.

With the help of some friendly crows, Timothy convinces Dumbo he can fly with the aid of a magic feather. During a performance, Dumbo loses the feather, but recovers his confidence in time to strike back at his tormentors, become a media sensation, and rescue his mother from her imprisonment.

Behind the Animation

- For its December 29, 1941, cover, *Time* magazine planned to feature Dumbo as "Mammal of the Year" (parodying "Man of the Year"), but the idea was cancelled due to the attack earlier that month on Pearl Harbor. *Time* used a photo of General Douglas MacArthur instead.

- The name of the circus seen on a blue-and-pink sign on a white building as the train leaves is "WDP Circus", standing for Walt Disney Productions. Sarasota, Florida, was the winter home for John Ringling's Greatest Show on Earth beginning in 1927, which is why the WDP Circus is there as well.

- RKO Pictures, the distributor of the Disney cartoons, tried desperately to persuade Walt to add more time to the 64-minute feature, but Walt insisted that it was perfect just as it was.

- "Jumbo" is a reference to the famous Barnum and Bailey African circus elephant who was the largest elephant in captivity and the first international animal superstar.

- The Hall Johnson Choir, a highly esteemed black singing group from Harlem, provided the voices for the crows, except for leader Jim Crow which was voiced by Cliff Edwards (the voice of Jiminy Cricket) who had done a black dialect act in vaudeville.

Quotable Quotes

The very things that hold you down are going to lift you up.
— Timothy Mouse

I think I been done seen everything when I see an elephant fly.
— The Crows

After all, one mustn't forget one is a lady.
— Matriarch of the Elephants

The magic feather was just a gag. You can fly!
— Timothy Mouse

Bambi (1942)

The film follows the life of a deer named Bambi from his birth to learning how to balance on wobbly legs on an icy lake to discovering the forest and making new friends like Thumper the rabbit, Flower the skunk, and Faline, a female fawn.

The first winter brings the loss of Bambi's mother from a hunter's rifle. As the friends grow into young adulthood, the wise old owl warns them about "twitterpation" as they all fall in love. Bambi earns Faline's affection by battling an angry older stag named Ronno who has tried to claim her as his mate.

Shortly afterward, the forest is accidentally set aflame by a careless hunter's campfire. In the ensuing panic and destruction, Bambi is separated from Faline. He finally finds her cornered by vicious hunting dogs and rescues her. The pair along with many of the other forest animals find refuge on a riverbank as the forest is destroyed. The following spring, a time of rebirth, Faline gives birth to twins while Bambi assumes his inherited role as the new Great Prince of the Forest.

Behind the Animation

- "Man is in the forest" was the same phrase that some of the Disney animators used to alert others that Walt Disney was wandering the Disney Studio.

- None of the songs in the film are sung by any of the characters, but by an unseen forty voice chorus. The song "Love is a Song" and the score were both nominated for Oscars.

- Bambi and his friends were used for the original poster for the "Only You Can Prevent Forest Fires" campaign in 1944. The Forest Service was so pleased with the results that on August 9, 1944, they authorized the creation of Smokey Bear. The first poster was delivered on October 10 of that year by artist Albert Stahle.

- Avid outdoorsman and Disney animator Jake Day arranged for two four-month-old fawns to model for Bambi and Faline. They took a four-day train ride from Maine to the Disney Studio in Hollywood. During the time they were being sketched at the studio, the fawns lost their spots and grew into adulthood, and were released in Griffith Park.

- Animator Marc Davis combined the facial aspects of a real deer with those of a human baby to create the look for the young Bambi.

Quotable Quotes

Everything in the forest has its season. Where one thing falls, another grows. Maybe not what was there before, but something new and wonderful all the same.

— Bambi's Mother

···

Nearly everybody gets twitterpated in the springtime. For example: You're walking along, minding your own business. You're looking neither to the left, nor to the right, when all of a sudden you run smack into a pretty face. Woo-woo!

You begin to get weak in the knees. Your head's in a whirl. And then you feel light as a feather, and before you know it, you're walking on air. And then you know what? You're knocked for a loop, and you completely lose your head!

And that ain't all. It could happen to anyone, so you'd better be careful.

— Friend Owl

···

If you can't say something nice...don't say nothing at all.

— Thumper

···

Love is a song that never ends.

— "Love is a Song" lyric

Saludos Amigos (1943)

Saludos Amigos was the first anthology or "package" film that, instead of telling one long narrative, presented instead a collection of short cartoons.

Originally, Walt Disney intended to make a series of short animated cartoons with each spotlighting individual South American countries in an effort to promote good will. He was later convinced it would be more effective to combine them into one film.

The four animated films, connected by live-action footage of Walt and the Disney artists in the actual South American countries gathering material for the films, include Donald Duck as an American tourist in Lake Titicaca who bumbles through the strange customs and has an unfortunate encounter with a condescending llama; a trip to Santiago, Chile, where a young anthropomorphic airplane named Pedro decides to do his ailing father's job of delivering mail through tough storm conditions over the Andes Mountains; affable Goofy demonstrating the life and culture of an Argentinean gaucho with his ever-faithful horse on the pampas; and Donald Duck, in Rio de Janeiro, meeting native Brazilian parrot José "Joe" Carioca who shows him the sights and sounds of the region with watercolor imagery and the captivating rhythm of the samba dance.

Behind the Animation

- The film was the first Hollywood movie to premiere in all Latin American countries (August 24, 1942) before opening in the United States (February 6, 1943). It was so popular in South America that *Collier's* magazine reported some audiences were "threatening to tear down the theater if they didn't repeat the film immediately after a showing".

- "Saludos Amigos" translates roughly to "Greetings Friends".

- The voice of Jose Carioca was provided by Jose Oliveira, a Brazilian musician who had directed singer Carmen Miranda's orchestra for ten years. The word "carioca" means native citizen of Rio de Janiero.

- In the movie, the footage of Walt and his team boarding the plane in the beginning had to be shot after they had returned from their trip since no one had filmed the actual boarding. They all dressed in the same outfits that they had worn when they first left.

- The little plane Pedro discovers there is only one postcard in his mail sack. The postcard was addressed to "Jorge Delano", the cartoonist who was the Santiago, Chile, guide for Walt and his artists. The postcard is from "Juan Carlos", who hosted a party in Mendoza for Walt's group before their flight to Santiago.

Quotable Quotes

A new day's waiting to start; you must meet it, wake up and greet it, with a gay song in your heart!

— "Saludos Amigos" lyric

....

The people here are divided into two classes: those who walk against the wind and those who walk with the wind.

— Narrator: "Lake Titicaca"

....

It was built to withstand the fury of the elements. In fact, it seems to be impervious to practically everything except the inquisitive tourist.

— Narrator: "Lake Titicaca"

....

And above all, one should never lose one's temper.

— Narrator: "Lake Titicaca"

The Three Caballeros (1945)

Donald Duck opens a package from his Latin American friends filled with films and books for his upcoming birthday.

The first film is the story of Pablo, the cold-blooded South Pole penguin who suffers through many attempts to find a warmer home and then changes his mind; the second film introduces the wacky but pleasant Aracuan Bird who seems to defy all natural laws; "The Flying Gauchito" is the tale of a young boy who has captured a winged burrito that can fly and tries to use him to win a horse race; and finally there's a pop-up book on Brazil that re-introduces Joe Carioca who takes Donald to Baia (Bahia), featuring a live-action interlude with Aurora Miranda, sister of the famous singer Carmen Miranda.

This adventure leads to the appearance of Mexican rooster Panchito and a cleverly animated rendition of the title song, followed by a lesson about the Las Posadas Christmas tradition, a magic serape ride across Mexico, and live-action interactions with singers Dora Luz, Carmen Molina, and a beach filled with flirty young women in swim suits.

A battle between Donald and a toy bull loaded with fireworks brings the film to an explosive conclusion.

Behind the Animation

- The world premiere for the film was held in Mexico City on December 21, 1944. Carmen Molina and Dora Luz appeared onstage at the premiere. It was released in the United States on February 3, 1945.

- The title song, "The Three Caballeros", is based on the melody of a Mexican song "Ay, Jalisco, no te rajes!"composed by Manuel Esperón. Walt Disney asked him personally to participate in the movie and new English lyrics were written for the song by Ray Gilbert.

- A group of Disney Studio artists visited Mexico from late 1942 through early 1943, auditioning Mexican performers and making sketches and paintings to be used as reference material. Another trip was taken in July 1943.

- While aerial live-action shots of an Acapulco beach were photographed, the scene of the bathing beauties interacting with Donald Duck was filmed on the Disney Studio parking lot covered with sand during January and February 1944.

- Panchito was voiced by nightclub singer Joaquin Garay after more than a hundred other actors were tested. His son Joaquin Garay III played the major role of Paco in the 1980 Disney live-action film, *Herbie Goes Bananas*.

Quotable Quotes

Through fair or stormy weather, we stand close together like books on the shelf.
— "The Three Caballeros" lyric

When I said "I love you", every beat of my heart said it, too.
— "You Belong To My Heart" lyric

Never satisfied. That's human nature for you.
— Narrator: "The Cold-Blooded Penquin"

Believe it or not, it is very simple.
— Jose Carioca

Make Mine Music (1946)

Another package film that includes a story of the classic feuding hillbillies known as the Martins and the Coys; a mood piece set on a blue bayou in the Everglades; a jazz segment called "All the Cats Join In" showcasing Benny Goodman and his orchestra that focuses on a group of lively bobby-soxers; a ballad of lost love entitled "Without You"; a spirited telling of the classic Ernest Thayer poem "Casey at the Bat", about a baseball hero; "Two Silhouettes", with ballet dancers performing in silhouette; and "Peter and the Wolf", an animated dramatization of the 1936 musical composition by Sergei Prokofiev narrated by Sterling Holloway.

The film also has "After You've Gone", featuring anthropomorphized musical instruments romping through a surreal landscape; "Johnnie Fedora and Alice Bluebonnet", telling the story of two hats who fall in love in a department store, are separated, but eventually reunite for a happy ending; and finally "The Whale Who Wanted to Sing at the Met", about Willie, a real sperm whale who can sing opera, but a famous operatic impresario mistakenly believes the mammal has swallowed three opera singers and kills the creature with a harpoon to rescue them.

Behind the Animation

- The animated short "The Martins and the Coys" was cut from the American VHS and DVD release of the film because of concerns over excessive comic gunplay. It remains intact on the U.K. version.

- Singer Nelson Eddy voiced Willie the Whale and tinkered with his home recording equipment so he was able, according to Disney Studio publicity, " to sing the complete score and, by changing the register of his voice at will, to be in turn a soprano, tenor, baritone and bass—then all four at once".

- Animation in "Blue Bayou" was originally intended to be used to accompany Claude Debussy's composition "Clair de Lune" for the film *Fantasia* (1940).

- U.K. censors demanded that depictions of "Sonia the Duck" and "Willie the Whale" as angels be cut, in addition to the shot of the Pearly Gates with a "sold out" sign at the end of the segment featuring Willie.

- At the time of the film's release, Walt Disney told reporters that because the studio could not obtain the rights to use music from the opera *I Pagliacci* for the Willie the Whale segment, singer Nelson Eddy "wrote a phony one himself. Complete with sobs."

Quotable Quotes

Miracles never really die.
> — Narrator: "The Whale That Wanted to Sing at the Met"

···

You could see that love had kicked him in the face.
> — "The Martins and the Coys" song lyric

···

And here am I still haunted by the ghost of long ago.
> — "Blue Bayou" song lyric

···

Two hearts on fire will soon inspire the stars to dance.
> — "Two Silhouettes" song lyric

Fun and Fancy Free (1947)

Interestingly, Jiminy Cricket hosts this film. The first story is Sinclair Lewis' tale of Bongo, a performing circus bear who dreams of being out in the wild, but when he escapes, he finds it is much different than what he imagined. He encounters a beautiful girl bear named Lulubelle and is forced to use his skills to battle his enormous rival bear Lumpjaw to win her.

The second story is ventriloquist Edgar Bergen and his dummy sidekicks, Charlie McCarthy and Mortimer Snerd, telling young actress Luana Patten the story of "Jack and the Beanstalk" featuring Mickey Mouse, Donald Duck, and Goofy. When Willie the Giant steals the singing golden harp, Happy Valley is not so happy anymore.

The desperate trio trades their beloved cow for a handful of magic beans from which sprout a beanstalk to a land in the clouds where Willie has a castle. Comic misadventures ensue and Mickey, Donald, and Goofy are able to return the singing harp, and happiness, to Happy Valley.

The cartoon ends with Willie the Giant (having survived the fall from the beanstalk) stomping through Hollywood looking for Mickey Mouse and surprising the live-action storytellers.

Behind the Animation

- Voice actor Billy Gilbert was known for comedic sneezing. He provided the voice of the hapless Willie and also supplied the voice for Sneezy in *Snow White and the Seven Dwarfs* (1937). Willie has a huge, important sneeze in the film.

- A scene of Mickey Mouse trading the cow to the Queen, portrayed by Minnie Mouse, was storyboarded and a voice track recorded, but the sequence was never animated.

- Jiminy Cricket's opening song, "I'm a Happy-Go-Lucky Fellow", was originally recorded for the 1940 Disney animated feature *Pinocchio* (1940), but was not used.

- *Fun and Fancy Free* was released in September in conjunction with the celebration of Mickey Mouse's birthday in several theaters. One party screening held at the Disney Studio in October was attended by Edgar Bergen's young daughter Candice and the children of other celebrities.

- This is the feature film debut of Disney sound effects man Jimmy MacDonald doing the voice of Mickey Mouse. Walt had recorded some of Mickey's lines as early as 1941, but got too busy to complete the task.

Quotable Quotes

Just learn to smile, and in a while, you'll find trouble's a bubble of air.

— Jiminy Cricket

....

You know, you worry too much. In fact, everybody worries too much.

— Jiminy Cricket

....

Here, just look at the morning paper. Turn to any page. You'll find the whole world worryin' about some future age. But why get so excited? What's gonna be is gonna be. The end of the world's been comin' since 1903. That's, uh, B.C., of course.

— Jiminy Cricket

....

In my favorite dream, everyone is so delightful; no one's mean or spiteful.

— The Golden Harp

Melody Time (1948)

Another package film. Its seven segments include "Once Upon a Wintertime", featuring two young lovers who are rescued from an icy river by clever animals; "Bumble Boogie", a swing-jazz piano version of the famous Rimsky-Korsakov's composition "Flight of the Bumblebee" with a frantic solo bee avoiding peril; a fanciful retelling of the legend of John "Johnny Appleseed" Chapman, who spent his life roaming Illinois and Indiana planting apple trees during the pioneer days; a segment based on Hardie Gramatky's children's story about a tugboat named Little Toot who grows up from playing pranks to saving the day; Joyce Kilmer's famous poem "Trees", set to music; and "Blame It On the Samba" which reunites Joe Carioca, Donald Duck, and the Aracuan Bird as they are engulfed in the rhythm of the samba.

In addition, the most prominent segment has young actors Bobby Driscoll and Luana Patten listening intently as Roy Rogers and the Sons of the Pioneers tell the colorful story of the legendary Pecos Bill and how he met and almost married Slue Foot Sue.

Behind the Animation

- Bobby Driscoll and Luana Patten also appeared together in the Disney feature films *Song of the South* (1946) and *So Dear to My Heart* (1949).

- The National Apple Institute did advertising to help promote the Johnny Appleseed segment and claimed it would prompt an additional three million people to buy tickets for the film.

- Starting in 2000, in an attempt at political correctness for American audiences, Disney digitally removed the cigarette dangling from Pecos Bill's lips in every frame and removed the segments with the cyclone and the painted desert Indians. Foreign releases remain uncensored.

- Hardie Gramatky worked at the Disney Studio as an animator beginning in late 1929 and left in 1936. "Little Toot", written and illustrated by Gramatky, was first published in 1939. When Capitol Records produced a record with the Little Toot song from this film, it was the first children's record to hit the 1,000,000 sales mark on Billboard.

- Pinto Colvig, the original voice of Goofy and Grumpy, provided the voice and singing for the Aracuan bird in this film, in *The Three Caballeros* (1945), and in the short *Clown of the Jungle* (1947).

Quotable Quotes

The Lord is good to me and so I thank the Lord for giving me the things I need, the sun and rain and an apple seed.

— Johnny Appleseed

He was the roughest, toughest critter, never known to be a quitter 'cuz he never had no fear of man or beast.

— Roy Rogers and the Sons of the Pioneers singing about Pecos Bill

So if three boisterous birds of a feather fall under the influence of this torrid tropical tempo, don't blame them, blame it on the rhythm of the samba.

— Narrator: "Blame it on the Samba"

"There's poetry in trees, they say, and one day a poet found it.

— Narrator: "Trees"

The Adventures of Ichabod and Mr. Toad (1949)

The film is a compilation of two stories that Walt Disney had considered developing into separate features: "The Legend of Sleepy Hollow", inspired by Washington Irving's story, and "The Wind and the Willows", based on Kenneth Grahame's novel.

Ichabod Crane, the superstitious and awkward new schoolteacher in town, has taken a fancy to wealthy Katrina van Tassel, much to the dismay of her oafish suitor, Brom Bones. At a late-night Halloween party, Brom frightens Ichabod with the tale of a headless horseman who roams the land looking for a new head. On his ride home, Ichabod encounters the horseman and a wild chase ends with the disappearance of Ichabod from Tarrytown.

J. Thaddeus Toad, Esq. is a happy-go-lucky wealthy gentleman who is obsessed with having fun and new adventures to the detriment of his financial responsibilities. His mania for an automobile gets him in trouble, including being arrested for theft and losing the deed to his mansion to some weasels and an unscrupulous bartender named Mr. Winkie. His sensible friends, Ratty, Moley, and MacBadger, as well as his horse Cyril Proudbottom, help Toad reclaim his rightful heritage.

Behind the Animation

- Brom Bones was one of the inspirations for Gaston in *Beauty and the Beast* (1991).

- Just like with *Fun and Fancy Free* (1947), it was originally planned that Jiminy Cricket would introduce these stories under the title "Two Fabulous Characters".

- In 1948, it was announced that Bing Crosby's four sons would be filmed in live action gathered around a radio listening to their father's voice telling the tale of the Headless Horseman. The Crosby family would receive five percent of the gross revenue from the film up to $200,000 in lieu of a straight salary. This introduction was never filmed.

- Walt acquired the rights to *Wind in the Willows* in June 1938 and a basic script and the song "We're Merrily on Our Way" were ready in 1941, but Walt put the project on hiatus in October of that year. Animation started back up in 1945.

- Disney Legend Blaine Gibson specifically requested to animate on the scene of a scared Ichabod riding his horse into Sleepy Hollow because it reminded him of an incident when he was boy on a farm in eastern Colorado.

Quotable Quotes

Don't try to figure out a plan. You can't reason with a headless man.
— "The Headless Horseman" song lyric

••

We're merrily, merrily, merrily, merrily on our way to nowhere in particular.
— Mr. Toad

••

Weasels I know are deceiving and not to be trusted at all.
— Cyril Proudbottom

••

No good can ever come about from traveling with such a fast and irresponsible beast.
— Ratty

Cinderella (1950)

Before his death, Ella's father marries the conniving Lady Tremaine who had two daughters named Anastasia and Drizella. They take control of the estate and treat Ella as a housekeeping servant. They cruelly nickname her "Cinderella" because she is sometimes covered with cinders from lying near the fireplace for warmth. Her only friends are the birds, mice, a horse, and a dog who repay her many kindnesses with their friendship.

A royal decree announces a ball to be attended by all eligible maidens so the prince can find a wife. Cinderella rushes to complete all her chores and the animals help in making her a dress from her mother's old gown so she can attend, but her step-sisters rip it to shreds just as they are all leaving.

A fairy godmother appears to the despairing young girl, and with her magic creates a horse-drawn carriage, servants, and beautiful dress with glass slippers that will all vanish at the stroke of midnight. At the ball, Cinderella wins the young prince's heart, but races out from the ball at midnight, forcing the noble to hunt throughout the land for the maiden who left a single glass slipper behind. The two marry and live happily ever after.

Behind the Animation

- The prince's name is never mentioned in the film, nor is he ever referred to as "Prince Charming". Singer and television talk show host Mike Douglas provided the singing voice for the prince. William Phillips did the speaking voice because of Douglas' strong Chicago accent.

- Big Band-era singer Ilene Woods was selected over three hundred other young female singers, including Dinah Shore, for the role of Cinderella.

- *Cinderella* was the first Disney animated feature to be filmed almost completely in live action before animation began to save time and money in determining camera angles, editing, and movement.

- This was the first animated feature to contain animation work from all of the "Nine Old Men". The scene animated by Marc Davis of Cinderella getting her ball gown from the Fairy Godmother was Walt's favorite piece of animation.

- Actress Helene Stanley was the live-action reference model for Cinderella and for Anastasia Tremaine. She later modeled for Princess Aurora in *Sleeping Beauty* (1959) and Anita Radcliffe in *101 Dalmatians* (1961).

Quotable Quotes

Even miracles take a little time.
— The Fairy Godmother

A dream is a wish your heart makes when you're fast asleep.
— Cinderella

Have faith in your dreams and some day, your rainbow will come smiling through.
— Cinderella

If you keep on believing, the dream that you wish will come true.
— Cinderella

Alice in Wonderland (1951)

The film contains elements from both Lewis Carroll's famous novel *Alice's Adventures in Wonderland* and its sequel *Through the Looking Glass*.

On a golden summer afternoon in an English countryside, a bored young girl named Alice follows a frantic clothed white rabbit down a rabbit hole and finds herself in the madcap world of Wonderland.

In her efforts to find the rabbit as well as return home, she constantly changes sizes and encounters a wide variety of odd and frustrating characters, including the brothers Tweedledee and Tweedledum; a singing garden of pompous flowers; a haughty questioning caterpillar; the mysterious Cheshire Cat who is always smiling and disappearing; the wacky Mad Hatter, March Hare, and Dormouse at an Unbirthday Tea Party; and talking playing cards.

Unfortunately, she also encounters the tyrannical Queen of Hearts, and after an unfortunate incident during a croquet match with her majesty, Alice finds herself put on trial. The Queen orders Alice decapitated, but the clever girl escapes and just as she is about to be overcome by all the forces of Wonderland, she finds that it was all just a dream and rejoins her older sister by the riverbank.

Behind the Animation

- The talking Doorknob is the only character in the film not to appear in any of Carroll's books. He was voiced by Joseph Kearns who later portrayed the neighbor "Mr. Wilson" in the *Dennis the Menace* television series.

- *Alice* is the first Disney animated feature where the voice talent is credited on screen, perhaps because some of the voices like Ed Wynn and Jerry Colona were well-known celebrities.

- Walt brought in Aldous Huxley, author of *Brave New World*, who came up with a version of the script that mixed a live-action story about Charles Dodgson (who wrote under the "Carroll" pseudonym) and three animated sequences taking place in Wonderland.

- Over the years, Walt had considered making the story of Alice with a live-action actress like Mary Pickford, Ginger Rogers, or Luana Patten interacting with animated characters, just as he had done in the "Alice Comedies" short cartoons.

- In the opening credits, Lewis Carroll's last name is incorrectly spelled with only one "L" and his book is incorrectly identified as "The Adventures of Alice in Wonderland".

Quotable Quotes

Nothing's impossible.

— Doorknob

•••

It would be so nice if something would make sense for a change!

— Alice

•••

But that's just the trouble with me. I give myself very good advice, but I very seldom follow it.

— Alice

•••

I have an excellent idea, LET'S CHANGE THE SUBJECT.

— March Hare

Peter Pan (1953)

Based on James Barrie's popular novel, the film version has Peter Pan visiting a London nursery to hear stories and then taking the teenage storyteller, Wendy Darling, and her two younger brothers, John and Michael, to his home in Neverland. Thanks to happy thoughts and a little pixie dust from Peter's fairy companion, Tinker Bell, they are able to fly there.

They meet the Lost Boys, an Indian tribe, and some mermaids. The adventure of never growing up is marred by their encounters with Captain Hook and his menacing pirate crew that are out to put an end to Peter for feeding Hook's hand to a crocodile who now longs for the rest of his meal.

Wendy and her brothers get homesick and offer to take the Lost Boys home with them. They are all captured by Hook and his men and taken to his ship, where he intends to make them the newest members of his crew or have them walk the plank. Peter has remained behind and barely escapes being blown up by a bomb left by Hook. Peter quickly flies to the ship and rescues everyone after a thrilling battle with the pirate captain. He then takes Wendy and her brothers home.

Behind the Animation

- This is the only version of the story where Hook's hook is on the left hand because the animators felt that the right hand would be more expressive. Peter cuts off Hook's right hand in the novel because it's the one holding the sword that's poking him.

- As a young boy, Walt Disney played Peter Pan in a school play. His older brother Roy held the rope that was allowing him to fly, but Walt was so enthusiastic in the air that he ended up falling into the front row of seats.

- Actor Bobby Driscoll, who voiced Peter and was the live-action reference model for the character (as was dancer Roland Dupree), is generally considered the first male to portray the role that was traditionally performed by a woman. This was his last role in a Disney film.

- *Peter Pan* was Michael Jackson's favorite Disney animated feature. He named his ranch in Santa Barbara, California, "Neverland" and commissioned Disney artists to draw him as Peter Pan.

- This film was the last Disney animated feature where all "Nine Old Men" worked on it as directing animators.

Quotable Quotes

All it takes is faith and trust. Oh! And something I forgot. Dust! Yep, just a little bit of pixie dust. Now, think of the happiest things. It's the same as having wings.

— Peter Pan

A jealous female can be tricked into anything.
— Captain Hook

A pirate's life is a wonderful life. You'll find adventure and sport. But live every minute. For all that is in it, the life of a pirate is short.
— Unnamed Pirate

All this has happened before, and it will all happen again.

— Narrator

Lady and The Tramp (1955)

On Christmas morning, Jim Dear gives his wife, Darling, a baby cocker spaniel that they name "Lady". As Lady grows up, she makes friends with two neighborhood dogs: Jock, a Scottie, and Trusty, a bloodhound.

Lady worries that the upcoming birth of a baby for her owners may steal their love for her. This fear is reinforced by a street-smart stray mongrel named Tramp whose roguish charms eventually capture her affections.

With the arrival of Aunt Sarah and her two Siamese cats to help care for the new baby, Lady finds herself literally in the outside doghouse and wearing a muzzle. She is rescued by Tramp who takes her on a romantic night on the town, including a memorable spaghetti dinner, but they end up at the pound. Lady is retrieved and chained in the back yard, so she is unable to protect the baby from a large rat.

Hearing her barks, Tramp returns and kills the rat just in time, but a confused Sarah sends him away with the dogcatcher. Jock and Trusty desperately rush after the wagon, forcing it to crash.

By Christmas, Tramp has been adopted by the family and is the father of three daughters and a son.

Behind the Animation

- Giving a gift of a puppy in a hatbox at Christmas was based on an actual incident in Walt Disney's life where he gave a Chow puppy to his wife, Lillian, in the same manner.

- A real rat was kept in a cage on animator Woolie Reitherman's desk for him to study for the fight finale. People were sent out to the docks at San Pedro to try and capture a vicious wharf rat, but had to settle for a tame one from a pet store.

- Singer Peggy Lee sued the Disney Company claiming that she had only signed away her rights for the movie and the soundtrack, but not other media such as videos. After a lengthy court battle, she was finally awarded $2.3 million in damages in 1991.

- *Lady and the Tramp* was the first feature-length animated movie to be made simultaneously both in CinemaScope and in the standard aspect ratio.

- Background artist Claude Coats built a complete miniature replica of the Dear's Victorian Gothic home, furnished and decorated, in order to help animators get a "dog's eye view" and choose some interesting angles.

Quotable Quotes

Look, there's a great big hunk of world down there with no fence around it where two dogs can find adventure and excitement, and beyond those distant hills, who knows what wonderful experiences? And it's all ours for the taking.
— Tramp

* * *

Side by side with your loved one, you'll find enchantment here. The night will weave its magic spell, when the one you love is near.
— "Bella Notre" song lyric

* * *

When you're footloose and collar-free, well, you take nothing but the best.
— Tramp

* * *

Lady: "But we shouldn't."

Tramp: "I know. That's what makes it fun. Start building some memories."

Sleeping Beauty (1959)

Princess Aurora is born. Three good fairies named Flora, Fauna, and Merryweather attend the christening. The ceremony is interrupted by the dark fairy Maleficent, who curses the child so that before sunset on her sixteenth birthday, she will prick her finger on the spindle of a spinning wheel and die.

Fortunately, Merryweather has not yet granted her gift and so modifies the curse so that the princess will only appear dead, but can be awakened by true love's first kiss. The three good fairies spirit the child away to the forest where they raise her as their own until the fateful day.

While gathering berries in the forest, Briar Rose, as she is now known, encounters the charming Prince Phillip, and they instantly fall in love.

Thanks to her raven's cleverness, Maleficent is there when the girl returns to the castle and fulfills the curse. The fairies put the entire kingdom under a spell of sleep until Briar Rose/Aurora awakens.

Maleficent also captures the prince, but with the help of the fairies he escapes her dungeon. An enraged Maleficent beats him to the castle and transforms into a terrifying dragon that he defeats. He finds Aurora and his kiss awakens her and the entire kingdom.

Behind the Animation

- Actress Eleanor Audley, who provided the distinctive voice for Maleficent, was battling tuberculosis at the time and initially turned down the offer. She also provided the voice for Lady Tremaine in *Cinderella* (1950) and Madame Leota in the Haunted Mansion attraction at the Disney parks.

- To create the sound of the dragon's fiery breath, Disney sound effects expert Jim Macdonald contacted the United States Army for some training films on flame throwing. Castanets were used for the sound of the dragon's snapping jaws.

- Warner Bros' animator and director Chuck Jones worked on the film for about three months on the three fairies before deciding that the atmosphere at the Disney Studio was not conducive to his way of working.

- *Sleeping Beauty* was the last Disney animated feature to have cels inked by hand. Some of the cels were done by the xerography process.

- The book used in the beginning of the film to introduce the story was real. It was made by hand by artist Eyvind Earle who was in charge of the overall artistic design of the film.

Quotable Quotes

It can only do good, dear, to bring joy and happiness.
— Fauna the Fairy

Oh...I just love happy endings.
— Fauna the Fairy

The road to true love may be barred by still many more dangers, which you alone will have to face.
— Flora the Fairy

Maleficent doesn't know anything about love, or kindness, or the joy of helping others. You know, sometimes I don't think she's really very happy.
— Fauna the Fairy

101 Dalmatians (1961)

Songwriter Roger Radcliffe lives in a London bachelor flat with his Dalmatian, Pongo. On a walk, they meet Anita and her Dalmatian, Perdita, and both couples fall in love and marry. After Perdita gives birth to a litter of fifteen puppies, Roger and Anita are visited by one of Anita's old schoolmates, wealthy Cruella De Vil, who wants to buy them all, but is refused.

Cruella hires Horace and Jasper to dognap the puppies, and Scotland Yard is unable to help.

Fortunately, the dog community has a communication system known as the Twilight Bark, so Pongo and Perdita are able to locate their children along with 84 additional Dalmatian puppies held at the supposedly abandoned De Vil estate. Cruella intends to skin the entire lot to make into a coat.

Pongo and Perdita rescue all the puppies and try to make their way home to London through deep snow, with Cruella and her henchmen in hot pursuit. Fortunately, the villains are all involved in a massive car accident. When the dogs are reunited with Roger and Anita, who have made quite a bit of money from Roger's song about Cruella, it is decided to open a Dalmatian Plantation in the country for all 101 dogs.

Behind the Animation

- The birth of fifteen Dalmatian puppies actually happened to author Dodie Stevens who wrote the book the film was based on. One was born lifeless, but her husband revived it just like in the film.

- All the black spots that appear on the dogs in the movie, frame-by-frame, total 6,469,952, or roughly 72 spots on Pongo, 68 on Perdita, and 32 on each pup. Lucky's spots on his back form a horseshoe, a symbol of good luck.

- Only six of the fifteen puppies have names: Lucky, Rolly, Patch, Penny, Pepper, and Freckles.

- Eight hundred gallons of special paint weighing nearly 5 tons were used in producing the animation cels and backgrounds—that's enough to cover 15 football fields or the outsides of 135 average homes. Nearly 1,000 different shades of color were created.

- Bill Peet, who wrote the script for *101 Dalmations*, was the first person to single-handedly write an entire Disney animated feature. Author Dodie Smith wrote "what a good storyline you achieved, very funny and very exciting and the humor never interferes with the suspense. I am more and more struck by the freshness of the film's new funny material which, to me, is exactly right."

Quotable Quotes

You've been thinking? Now look here, Horace! I warned you about thinking!

— Jasper

....

As far as I could see, the old notion that a bachelor's life was so glamorous and carefree was all nonsense. It was downright dull.

— Pongo

....

She's such a kind understanding soul. You know, at times she seems almost canine.

— Pongo

....

We're very honored to be of service. We're sorry we can't do more.

— The Cows

The Sword in The Stone (1963)

Very loosely adapted from T.H. White's 1938 novel of the same name, the film recounts the education of a twelve-year-old orphan nicknamed "Wart" who would eventually become King Arthur of England. He is guided to this goal by a rather flustered and grumpy wizard called Merlin.

Wart longs to be a knight's squire for his foster brother, Kay, but Merlin realizes the boy is destined for bigger things. Using his magic, he tutors the boy by transforming him into a fish (to learn about physics), a squirrel (to learn about gravity), and a sparrow when Archimedes the owl takes over the lessons and teaches Wart the joy of flying.

Disrupting the final lesson is the witch Madam Mim, who battles Merlin in a classic wizard's duel where the boy learns that brains, not magic, can win the day.

On New Year's Day, while performing his squire duties for a jousting tournament that will determine the new king of England, Wart forgets Kay's sword and pulls a nearby previously unmovable sword from an anvil as a replacement. When the disbelieving citizenry demands he do it again, he does so when others fail and becomes the rightful king.

Behind the Animation

- Storyman Bill Peet gave the character of Merlin some of Walt Disney's characteristics, including being cantankerous, demanding, playful, and intelligent. Physically, he gave Merlin the famous "Disney nose".

- Rickie Sorensen, Richard Reitherman, and Robert Reitherman (the last two the sons of the director Woolie Reitherman) all supplied the voice for Wart, because during the length of the production, their voices would change as they hit puberty.

- *The Sword in the Stone* was the first Disney animated feature to have songs by Richard Sherman and Robert Sherman. Two songs written for the film were cut before production began: "The Blue Oak Tree" and "The Magic Key". The latter was Merlin's lecture to Arthur about the value of an education and was replaced with "Higitus Figitus".

- Walt Disney first obtained the rights to this book in 1939 and the first storyboard was created in 1949. Walt was finally encouraged to put the film into production after seeing the 1960 Broadway production of the musical *Camelot*.

- When Mad Madam Mim is sitting at the table playing solitaire, she pulls the three of hearts from the deck; however, the three of hearts is already on the table.

Quotable Quotes

Who knows? Who knows anything?
— Archimedes the Owl

....

The best way to learn it is to do it.
— Archimedes the Owl

....

Don't you get any foolish ideas that magic will solve all your problems, because it won't.
— Merlin

....

That love business is a powerful thing. I'd say it's the greatest force on earth.
— Merlin

The Jungle Book (1967)

The Rudyard Kipling stories about Mowgli, a human boy who grows up in the jungles of India and is raised by a pack of wolves, was the basis for the film.

When the man cub turns ten years old, it is felt that he should be returned to the Man Village since the human-hating tiger Shere Khan has returned. The task is given to Bagheera the black panther, but Mowgli is determined to remain in the only world he has ever known.

He encounters Kaa, a hypnotic python who almost devours him twice; Colonel Hathi, leading a herd of elephants; the lovable Baloo the bear, who only worries about the bare necessities; and King Louie the orangutan, who wants to learn the secret of man's fire.

Shere Khan stalks the boy to kill him before he becomes a man. Baloo steps in to rescue Mowgli, but is injured. Mowgli then defeats Shere Khan by tying flaming branches to the tiger's tail that send him running off deep into the jungle. Finally taken to the Man Village, the reluctant Mowgli changes his mind when he sees a young girl at the nearby river fetching water and follows her back to civilization.

Behind the Animation

- *Jungle Book* was the first Disney animated feature to be released after Walt Disney's death and the last to be personally supervised by him. Walt acted out for animator Ollie Johnston how Baloo should move and came up with the idea for the ending.

- The four vultures in the film were going to be voiced by the musical group The Beatles and were designed to resemble them, with moptop haircuts. Scheduling conflicts and John Lennon's reluctance resulted in the characters being changed to a barbershop quartet.

- Voice artist Verna Felton performed as Winifred the elephant, her last work before her death. Her first vocal work for Disney was as the pompous elephant matron in *Dumbo* (1940).

- The only song not written by the Sherman Brothers for the film was "The Bare Necessities". It was written by Terry Gilkyson for an earlier version of the film and nominated for an Academy Award.

- To save money, animation in the finished film was recycled from *Song of the South* (1946), *The Adventures of Ichabod and Mr. Toad* (1949), *Goliath II* (1960), and *The Sword in the Stone* (1963). The dance of Baloo and King Louie would later be recycled in *Robin Hood* (1973) for Little John and Lady Kluck's dance.

Quotable Quotes

When you find out you can live without it and go along not thinking about it, I'll tell you something true: the bare necessities of life will come to you.

— Baloo

•••

Things will look better in the morning.

— Bagheera

•••

Look, Flaps, first I say, "What we gonna do?" Then you say, "I don't know, what you wanna do?" Then I say, "What we gonna do?" You say, "What you wanna do?" "What we gonna do?" "What you want..." Let's do SOMETHING!

Buzzie

•••

I can't be bothered with that, I have no time for that nonsense.

— Shere Khan

The Aristocats (1970)

In Paris, France, in 1910, an aging opera star named Madame Bonfamille draws up a will that states upon her death, her estate will go to her cat, Duchess, and her three kittens: painter Toulouse, pianist Berlioz, and romantic Marie. After their deaths, the remaining fortune would go to her faithful butler, Edgar.

Overhearing this information, Edgar decides to speed up the process by sedating the cats with sleeping pills and abandoning them in the countryside, where he is attacked by two hounds named Lafayette and Napoleon. When the cats awaken, they meet a carefree orange alley cat named Thomas O'Malley who is persuaded to guide them back to Paris.

Along their journey back home, they encounter two giddy geese as well as Scat Cat and his band of international jazz musician cats. Finally returning to Madame Bonfamille's house, the cats are once again captured by Edgar.

It is up to O'Malley, aided by the brave mouse Roquerfort, to save all of them and box up and send Edgar off to Timbuktu. Reunited with her beloved pets, Madame rewrites her will and establishes a charity for Parisian stray cats, and O'Malley becomes part of the Bonfamille household.

Behind the Animation

- The Sherman Brothers convinced singer Maurice Chevalier to come out of retirement briefly to record the title song that they had written. Chevalier did it because of his love of Walt Disney. It was the last work he did before his death in 1972.

- The story was originally intended to be a two-part, live-action movie for the weekly Disney television show with the animals talking, but not in front of humans. The premise of the story was based on an actual incident of cats at the turn-of-the century who inherited a fortune from their owner.

- The character of Scat Cat was designed to look like and be voiced by jazz legend Louis Armstrong including his physique, gap between his teeth, and unique way of playing the trumpet. Illness prevented him from doing the role.

- While the story had been approved by Walt Disney to be converted to an animated feature instead of live action , he died before the film went into actual production.

- The English geese Amelia and Abigail Gabble were voiced by Carole Shelley and Monica Evans. They had had great success playing the giddy English Pigeon sisters, both in the original Broadway play and in movie version of Neil Simon's *The Odd Couple*.

Quotable Quotes

Ladies don't start fights, but they can finish them!

— Marie

Everybody wants to be a cat because a cat's the only cat who knows where it's at.

— Scat Cat

Wait a minute. I'm the leader. I'll say when it's the end. It's the end.

— Napoleon

Females never fight fair!

— Toulouse

Robin Hood (1973)

Based on the well-known legend of the daring outlaw of Sherwood Forest who robbed from the rich and gave to the poor while being pursued by Prince John, the ruler of England, and his minion, the Sheriff of Nottingham, the story was retold using animal characters in the human roles.

When Robin learns from Friar Tuck that there will be a Golden Arrow archery tournament to acknowledge the best archer in the land, and that the prize will be a kiss from Maid Marian, he cannot resist, even though he knows it must be a trap. Robin wins the tournament, but his true identity is revealed and he is almost captured.

In retaliation, Prince John raises all the taxes and arrests Friar Tuck for treason and orders him to be executed, hoping to once again draw Robin out of hiding. Robin and Little John rescue the cleric along with others imprisoned unfairly, with Robin making a daring leap from the fiery castle into the moat below.

Later, King Richard returns, ousts his brother Prince John, and allows his niece Maid Marian to marry Robin, making an in-law out of an outlaw.

Behind the Animation

- As Lady Kluck charges through the field after the archery tournament, her actions resembling a football player are reinforced by a musical arrangement of "Fight On" and "On, Wisconsin", the respective fight songs of the University of Southern California and the University of Wisconsin.

- A few months before the film's release, the Disney Studio frantically searched around the world for international actor Peter Ustinov to return and re-record a few lines. It turned out Ustinov was working on a project in Burbank at the NBC studios a half mile away.

- Terry Jones of the Monty Python comedy troupe was originally considered to voice the character of Robin Hood, as was singer Tommy Steele.

- The character designs were done by Disney Legend Ken Anderson, and the concept of an animal head on what was basically a fur-covered human body helped inspire furry fandom.

- Country singer Roger Miller wrote and performed three of the five songs in the film as Allan-A-Dale the rooster, including "Whistle Stop" which was used in a speeded-up version for the popular Hamster Dance website.

Quotable Quotes

Keep your chin up, some day there will be happiness again.
— Robin Hood

If I tattletale, I'll die till I'm dead.
— Skippy

A mere slip of the forked tongue, Sire.
— Sir Hiss

You're mighty preachy and you're gonna preach your neck right into a hangman's noose.
— Sheriff of Nottingham

The Many Adventures of Winnie the Pooh (1977)

The film is a compilation of three twenty-five minute featurettes of the A.A. Milne characters made by Disney: *Winnie the Pooh and the Honey Tree* (1966), *Winnie the Pooh and the Blustery Day* (1968), and *Winnie the Pooh and Tigger Too* (1974).

Pooh's obsession with honey finds him disguising himself as a little black rain cloud to unsuccessfully get near a bee hive, and then he enters Rabbit's burrow to devour all the pots of honey. He gets stuck in the entrance until he loses some weight.

A blustery "Windsday" takes Pooh and Piglet to Owl's house for stories. Later, the appearance of Tigger introduces Pooh to the fear of Heffalumps and Woozles stealing his honey. A heavy rain causing flooding temporarily puts Pooh and Piglet in jeopardy, but is quickly resolved.

Rabbit makes an attempt to stop Tigger from constantly bouncing, but after Tigger and Roo get caught up a tree, it is agreed that Tigger's bouncing brings joy to the Hundred Acre Wood.

Extra material was created to link the three stories and to show the closure of Christopher Robin leaving Hundred Acre Wood and saying goodbye to Pooh.

Behind the Animation

- Walt Disney loved the scene of Rabbit decorating Pooh's stuck rear end when it sticks out into Rabbit's living room.

- For each of the original three shorts, the voice of Christopher Robin was performed by a different actor.

- *Winnie the Pooh and the Blustery Day* won the Academy Award for Best Animated Short Film. The Oscar was awarded posthumously to Walt Disney.

- Julie Andrews' then husband, Tony Walton, spent several hours explaining to the Sherman Brothers about the importance of the Pooh stories and their impact on British children growing up so the Shermans could better understand them.

- Tigger's trademark "Woo-hoo-hoo!" was ad-libbed by Paul Winchell, who did the sound in homage to the catch phrase of classic movie comedian Hugh Herbert. Winchell credited his British wife for giving him the inspiration for Tigger's signature phrase, TTFN ("Ta-ta for now"). In 1974, he earned a Grammy for Best Children's Recording with "The Most Wonderful Things About Tiggers" from the feature *Winnie the Pooh and Tigger Too*.

Quotable Quotes

What I like most of all is just doing nothing. When grown-ups ask, "What are you going to do?" and you say, "Nothing," and then you go and do it.

— Christopher Robin

....

It's not much of a tail, but I'm sort of attached to it.

— Eeyore

....

I don't mind the leaves that are leaving; it's the leaves that are coming.

— Piglet

....

Oh, stuff and fluff.

— Winnie the Pooh

The Rescuers (1977)

The Rescue Aid Society, an international organization of mice that meets in the basement of the United Nations building, finds a note in a bottle from a girl named Penny in need of help. Hungarian representative Miss Bianca and shy janitor Bernard are given the assignment to go and rescue her.

The girl has been kidnapped by pawn shop owner Madame Medusa and her bumbling henchman, Mr. Snoops, because of her small size. They hope to use her to retrieve the world's largest diamond, the Devil's Eye, hidden in a dark, narrow underground pirate cave in the Devil's Bayou that is constantly flooding.

The two mice engage Orville the albatross to fly them to the location where they enlist the help of the local animals including Evinrude the firefly to rescue Penny who is being guarded on an abandoned riverboat by Medusa's two huge pet alligators, Brutus and Nero.

Penny and the mice find the diamond, but Medusa takes it away and a wild melee ensues. Penny returns safely to New York where she donates the gem to the Smithsonian Museum and is finally adopted by a loving family. Bianca and Bernard are sent off on another adventure.

Behind the Animation

- The film was so popular it was almost made into a television series, but was replaced by *Chip 'n' Dale's Rescue Rangers* in 1989. It was the first Disney animated feature to have a sequel, *The Rescuers Down Under* (1990).

- Nearly 3.5 million copies of the VHS version of the film were recalled by Disney in 1999 due to a brief, blurry two-frame (out of 110,000 frames in the film) image of a topless woman in a window, which appears about 38 minutes into the movie.

- A calendar on Madame Medusa's back room wall states Thursday the 12th, meaning that finding the diamond and the rescue took place on Friday the 13th. Originally, Cruella De Vil was to play the part played by Madame Medusa.

- Mr. Snoops is a caricature of animation historian John Culhane, who was affectionately nicknamed "Mr. Snoops" for his investigative work at the studio. Rufus the cat is a caricature of animator and Disney Legend Ollie Johnston.

- The film won a Special Citation Award from the National Board of Review in the United States "for restoring and upgrading the art of animation".

Quotable Quotes

Well, an old codger like me could use a little ginger.

— Rufus

....

Always keep a little prayer in your pocket and you're sure to see the light.

"Someone's Waiting for You" song lyric

....

Faith is a bluebird, we see from afar. It's for real and as sure as the first evening star; you can't touch it, or buy it, or wrap it up tight, but it's there just the same, making things turn out right.

— Rufus

....

Madame Medusa: "You must gain their confidence...make them like you."

Snoops: "How do you do that?"

Madame Medusa: "You FORCE them to like you, idiot!"

The Fox and The Hound (1981)

Inspired by Daniel P. Mannix's 1967 novel, this is the story of the relationship between a fox and a hunting hound over a series of years.

A young orphaned fox is discovered by an owl named Big Mama who arranges for him to be cared for by kindly Widow Tweed who names him "Tod". The young hound Copper is owned by neighbor Amos Slade. While the fox and the hound are both children, they play and become friends.

After Slade takes Copper away during hunting season for training, he hesitates to resume the friendship with Tod when he returns. A train accident causes serious injuries to Slade's older dog, Chief, Copper's mentor, and Tod is blamed.

Copper swears vengeance and the widow releases Tod to the wild for his own safety where he initially struggles to fit in. Slade and Copper finally track him down and are attacked by a huge, vicious black bear. Tod leaps into the fray to protect Copper, and the three of them eventually tumble down a waterfall. When Slade prepares to shoot the exhausted fox, Copper rises to protect his friend and Slade backs off. The pair separate since they are natural enemies, but they remain friends.

Behind the Animation

- Tim Burton did some uncredited inbetweening animation on the long shots of Vixey, the female fox. Burton claimed that his work looked like "roadkill", even though the studio teamed him with Glen Keane to help him understand the Disney style.

- Glen Keane animated the climactic bear fight. His staging of the scene was inspired by Tramp battling the dogs in *Lady and the Tramp* (1955) animated by Woolie Reitherman.

- The film was delayed for almost a year when eleven Disney animators (roughly 17%) left during production to join Don Bluth and his new animation studio. Bluth had worked on animation of the Widow Tweed and her cow, Abigail, before leaving.

- John Lasseter's first animation on a Disney film was doing inbetweening on the introduction of Copper. He also did some work on Glen Keane's bear fight sequence.

- The National Stuttering Project protested the film's release on video because of a minor character that was a stammering woodpecker named Boomer. They also targeted Porky Pig.

Quotable Quotes

Darlin', forever is a long, long time, and time has a way of changing things.

— Big Mama

Goodbye may seem forever, farewell is like the end. But in my heart's a memory, and there you'll always be.

— Widow Tweed

If you give me a head start, I can beat you.

— Copper

If only the world wouldn't get in the way. If only people would just let you play.

— "Best of Friends" song lyric

The Black Cauldron (1985)

Based on Lloyd Alexander's book series, *The Chronicles of Prydain*, the story revolves around an assistant pig-keeper named Taran who dreams of being a knight and discovers that his pig, Hen Wen, is actually an oracle. The evil Horned King wants the pig to locate the fabled black cauldron that will unleash an invincible army of deathless warriors.

With the assistance of a magic sword, the pretty Princess Eilonwy, and the old minstrel Fflewddur Fflam, Taran strives to find and keep the black cauldron away from the Horned King. In the process, they encounter an unreliable and constantly hungry small creature named Gurgi, a world of tiny fairies known as the Fair Folk, and three conniving witches of Morva who give Taran the cauldron in exchange for his sword, leaving him no way of defeating the Horned King.

When the Horned King captures the three companions and the cauldron, he uses it to raise the dead. A heroic Gurgi sacrifices himself by jumping into the bubbling cauldron, destroying the undead army, the Horned King, and the castle. Taran trades the cauldron to the witches in exchange for reviving Gurgi, and they all return home.

Behind the Animation

- The first Disney animated feature to not contain any songs. The score for the film was composed by Elmer Bernstein who, while working on this film, was nominated for an Academy Award for his work on *Trading Places* (1983) and *Ghostbusters* (1984).

- *The Black Cauldron* was the first Disney animated feature to receive a PG rating and the last to be made at the Animation Building at the Disney Studio. The Animation Department was moved to a building in Glendale in December 1983.

- The management team at the Disney Studio changed during the production of this film, with new studio chairman Jeffrey Katzenberg so appalled by the film's length and graphic scenes that he cut out twelve minutes of finished animation before its release.

- The film rights to the five books in the series were obtained in 1973 and it took nearly five years of actual production beginning in 1980 and $25 million to complete the feature. Its domestic box office gross was barely $21 million.

- *The Black Cauldron* was the first film using the Walt Disney Pictures logo featuring a white silhouette of Sleeping Beauty castle in front of a clear blue background.

Quotable Quotes

Then you are a very foolish lad. Untried courage is no match for his evil. Just remember that.
— Dallben

Perhaps it would interest you to see what fate has in store for you.
— The Horned King

I was so hoping for someone who could help me escape.
— Princess Eilonwy

Eilonwy: "Aren't you charming!"
Gurgi: "And pungent, too."

The Great Mouse Detective (1986)

Inspired by the five *Basil of Baker Street* children's books, the basic conceit of two rodents closely modeled after Sherlock Holmes and Dr. Watson living under Holmes' residence was retained.

In 1897 London, Basil gets hired by Olivia Flaversham, a young mouse girl whose only parent, toymaker father Hiram, has been kidnapped before her eyes by a peg-legged bat. The bat, named Fidget, is the henchman of Basil's evil nemesis, Professor Ratigan, who plans to use the toymaker's skills to create a mechanical replica of the Queen of the Mice who will declare Ratigan the ruler of all Mousedom.

To stop this dastardly scheme, Basil and Olivia are joined by Dr. Dawson and Toby, a reliable and "real" rather than anthropomorphic Basset Hound. Unfortunately, Olivia is kidnapped, and Basil and Dawson find themselves in an elaborate spring loaded mousetrap device. Escaping just in time, they go to Buckingham Palace and save both Olivia and her father, thwarting Ratigan's plans.

A climactic battle inside the gears of Big Ben results in both Basil and Ratigan seemingly falling to their deaths, but Basil is saved at the last moment and returns with Dawson to his flat where a new case awaits them both.

Behind the Animation

- The voice of Sherlock Holmes in the film was taken from a 1966 Caedmon Records recording by actor Basil Rathbone, who was famous for playing the great detective in the movies.

- The clock tower scene was the first time that traditional hand-drawn characters were put in a computer-generated background. Layout artist Mike Peraza was inspired by a similar clock scene in Hayao Miyazkai's animated feature, *Castle of Cagliostro* (1979).

- Wanting to distance the film from Steven Spielberg's recent box office bomb, *Young Sherlock Holmes* (1985), Disney insisted that anything too British (including the title *Basil of Baker Street*) be removed.

- Songwriter Henry Mancini had written a parody of a Victorian British Music Hall tune that was already in rough animation and recorded by Shani Wallis. Jeffrey Katzenberg felt that it was not contemporary enough and brought in singer Melissa Manchester to write and perform the more upbeat "Let Me Be Good To You" for the pub scene.

- Dr. Dawson was fashioned in appearance and behavior after Eric Larson, one of Disney animation's fabled Nine Old Men. Larson was in charge of the animation training program at the studio for years and many of his former students worked on the film.

Quotable Quotes

There's always a chance, Doctor, as long as one can think.
— Basil of Baker Street

You should have chosen your friends more carefully.
— Ratigan

Isn't it clear to you? The superior mind has triumphed! I've won!
— Ratigan

I observe that there is a good deal of German music on the program. It is quite introspective, and I want to introspect.
— Sherlock Holmes

Oliver & Company (1988)

Inspired by Charles Dickens' *Oliver Twist*, this modern-day version features an orphaned kitten named Oliver on the streets of New York who teams up with a free-wheeling stray dog named Dodger and his band of canines who are clever thieves: Tito the Chihuahua, Einstein the Great Dane, Rita the Saluki, and Francis the Bulldog.

They are taken care of by a down-on-his-luck pickpocket named Fagin who has just three days to pay off his debts to a loan shark named Sykes. During an outing, Oliver accidentally gets adopted by a wealthy young girl named Jenny, much to the consternation of her pampered poodle Georgette. Fagin decides to hold Oliver for ransom to get the money he needs, but changes his mind when Jenny shows up.

However, Sykes kidnaps the girl to hold for a large ransom from her absent parents. Dodger rallies the dogs and with Oliver they rescue Jenny, but are confronted by Sykes' two vicious Dobermans. Fagin comes to the rescue on his scooter and a deadly chase ensues, ending in the deaths of Sykes and his dogs on a bridge.

Reunited, Jenny and Oliver hold a party at her home for the dogs and rejoice that Jenny's parents return tomorrow.

Behind the Animation

- Animators shot photos of New York streets as reference, using cameras set eighteen inches off the ground to get a dog's point of view. Dogs from previous Disney animated features, such as Peg, Trusty, Jock, and Pongo, make cameo appearances.

- Michael Eisner offered the role of Sykes to actor Marlon Brando, who turned it down because he thought the film would bomb.

- The song "Once Upon A Time in New York City" that plays at the beginning of the film was written by Barry Mann and Howard Ashman, making it Ashman's first song for a Disney animated feature.

- *Oliver & Company* was the first Disney film to have a department created especially for computer animation that included producing things like buildings, cars, trains, and Fagin's scooter.

- The film was also the first Disney animated feature to include product placement for brands like Coca-Cola, *USA Today*, Sony, and Ryder Truck Rental. It was all unpaid advertising to create a sense of reality in a New York setting.

Quotable Quotes

Pretty is nice, but still it's just pretty.
— Georgette

Perfect isn't easy.
— Georgette

This city's got a beat, and you gotta hook into it. And once you get the beat, you can do anything.
— Dodger

Isn't it rather dangerous to use one's entire vocabulary in a single sentence?
— Francis

The Little Mermaid (1989)

Inspired by Hans Christian Andersen's classic story, the film features a sixteen-year-old redheaded mermaid named Ariel who defies her father, King Triton, with her fascination for the surface world.

Her friends Flounder; a scatterbrained seagull named Scuttle; and her father's red crab adviser Sebastian can not dissuade the girl's curiosity, especially when she catches a glimpse of Prince Eric who she rescues from a storm. She makes a deal with the sea witch Ursula to exchange her voice for becoming a human. If Ariel does not receive true love's kiss by the end of the third day of having legs, she will join Ursula's garden of poor, unfortunate souls.

Ursula disguises herself as a young woman named Vanessa who has Ariel's voice and enchants Eric into marrying her the next day.

The ceremony is disrupted by Ariel and her friends, but it is too late for Ariel to fulfill her bargain. King Triton offers to take his daughter's place. Ursula uses his trident to enlarge herself and create a storm.

Eric heroically kills her with the bow of a decaying sunken ship, freeing all of Ursula's captives including a grateful Triton who returns Ariel to human form and blesses their marriage.

Behind the Animation

- There is a shot of Ariel sitting on a rock in a pose reminiscent of the iconic bronze Little Mermaid statue in Copenhagen harbor. There are thirteen replicas of the statue around the world.

- Ursula is considered part octopus because she has six tentacles as well as two human arms making a total of eight limbs. Ursula is the sister of Triton, a fact that was not officially revealed until the Broadway musical production.

- The film had more effects animation than any Disney animated feature since *Fantasia* (1940); nearly 80% of the film required effects work. Two-thirds of the film is set underwater and over a million bubbles were hand-drawn.

- Ben Wright, the voice of Grimsby, Eric's manservant, was also the voice of Rama, Mowgli's wolf father, in *The Jungle Book* (1967) and Dalmatian owner Roger Radcliffe in *101 Dalmatians* (1961). During the production of the film, no one knew until he told them. This was his last role.

- The name of Ariel's sister Atina was inspired by a musical that Alan Menken wrote called *Atina: Evil Queen of the Galaxy*; the second sister, Alana, was Howard Ashman's lyrical nod to Alan Menken; and the third sister, Andrina, was the name of one of the director's aerobics instructors.

Quotable Quotes

If I may say, far better than any dream girl is one of flesh and blood, one warm and caring, and right before your eyes.

— Grimsby

••

Looking around you'd think, "Sure, she's got everything." But who cares? No big deal. I want more.

— Ariel

••

Life's full of tough choices, isn't it?

— Ursula

••

Have I ever been wrong? I mean when it's important!

— Scuttle

The Rescuers Down Under (1990)

Miss Bianca and Bernard from *The Rescuers* (1977) reunite to save a young Australian boy and a majestic golden eagle from an evil poacher.

In the Australian Outback, Cody saves the life of a trapped giant eagle named Marahute and the grateful bird befriends him. Unfortunately, poacher Percival McLeach discovers the pair's connection and kidnaps Cody in hopes of discovering the location of the eagle. Alerted to the dire situation, Miss Bianca and Bernard engage the services of an albatross named Wilbur, the brother of Orville, to take them down under. Once there, they meet the flirtatious and capable Jake, an Australian mouse who becomes their guide.

Cody is trapped in a cage at McLeach's ranch along with other exotic animals. MacLeach tricks Cody into leading him to Marahute's nest and captures her. Her eggs have been hidden by Bernard, who orders Wilbur to guard them.

McLeach tries to feed Cody to the crocodiles to get rid of any evidence, but is foiled by Bernard's actions, and McLeach becomes the new meal for the deadly predators. Once Marahute is freed, she rescues both Cody and Bernard. Miss Bianca accepts Bernard's marriage proposal and Marahute's eggs hatch, heralding a happier future.

Behind the Animation

- This film was the first animated theatrical sequel ever made by Disney Animation, though its relative financial failure discouraged Disney from releasing further sequels theatrically. After the poor opening weekend box office, Jeffrey Katzenberg pulled all television advertisements for the film.

- There were plans for a third movie based on the characters, but, with the death in 1995 of Eva Gabor, who portrayed Miss Bianca, it was cancelled. Gabor also supplied the voice of Duchess the cat in *The Aristocats* (1970).

- McLeach's pet, Joanna, is a goanna, an Australian monitor lizard that can grow to an enormous size. The animators studied animals at the San Diego Zoo and some were brought to the studio for occasional modeling sessions. A three-foot-long monitor lizard named Little Dude posed for Joanna.

- Five members of the production team took a two-and-a half week, 4,000 mile research expedition around the Outback, returning with countless photographs and sketches. The opening scene includes the iconic Ayers Rock.

- The film was the first Disney animated feature to completely use the CAPS (Computer Animation Production System), a computer-based system used for ink and painting, rather than the traditional practice of hand painting.

Quotable Quotes

I didn't make it all the way through third grade for nothing.

— McLeach

Kids should be free! Free to run wild through the house on Saturday mornings, free to have cookies and milk, and get those little white mustaches, you know?

— Wilbur

Relax? I have never been more relaxed in my life! If I were any more relaxed, I'd be dead!

— Wilbur

It looks like Lady Luck has finally decided to smile on us. Everything's goin' our way!

— McLeach

Beauty and the Beast (1991)

A young arrogant prince is turned into a beast and his servants into living household items by an offended enchantress. He must learn to love and earn the love of someone in return, or remain a beast forever.

Ten years later, an inventor named Maurice loses his way in the forest and finds himself trapped in the Beast's castle. His young, book-loving daughter Belle offers to take his place, and the Beast accepts.

Her independent personality clashes with the creature, but they gradually start to bond over a period of time, thanks to Lumière the candlestick, Cogsworth the clock, and Mrs. Potts the teacup.

In Belle's village, a vain hunter named Gaston schemes to have Belle marry him by having her father committed to an asylum. When Belle returns to save her father, she reveals that a beast does indeed live in the nearby castle. Gaston inflames a mob to storm the place and kill the beast.

The Beast battles Gaston and spares his life, but the treacherous hunter mortally stabs the noble creature. Belle proclaims her love before the final rose petal falls, breaking the curse and transforming both the Beast and his household items back to human form.

Behind the Animation

- Belle is the only person in her village who wears blue to show she is different from everyone else. The Beast also wears blue so the audience will feel they belong together.

- The film is dedicated to songwriter Howard Ashman who died eight months before its release: "To our friend Howard, who gave a mermaid her voice and a beast his soul, we will be forever grateful."

- *Beauty and the Beast* was the first animated feature to be nominated for a Best Picture Academy Award. It lost to *The Silence of the Lambs* (1991). It was, however, the first full-length animated feature to win the Golden Globe for Best Picture (Musical or Comedy).

- The dance between Belle and her prince in the finale is actually traced animation of Princess Aurora and Prince Phillip dancing in *Sleeping Beauty* (1959). This was done because Disney animators were running out of time during the production.

- A song sung by the enchanted objects entitled "Human Again" was cut before production started and replaced by "Something There". The song was later added to the *Disney on Ice* show and the Broadway production of the film. It was recorded and animated for the 2001 IMAX re-release and 2002 special edition home video release.

Quotable Quotes

I want adventure in the great wide somewhere. I want it more than I can tell.

— Belle

We don't like what we don't understand. In fact, it scares us.

— "Mob" song lyrics

I let her go. I had to. Because I loved her.

— Beast

Beast: "I want to do something for her...but what?"

Cogsworth: "Well, there's the usual things: flowers...chocolates...promises you don't intend to keep..."

Aladdin (1992)

In the fictional Middle Eastern land of Agrabah, a street orphan named Aladdin survives through stealing.

The sultan's advisor, Jafar, uses his hypnotic influence to bend the sultan to his will. The sultan's daughter, Jasmine, is unhappy with her life behind the palace walls and on a clandestine trip to the marketplace is rescued by Aladdin. Aladdin is thrown in prison and Jafar uses the street rat to enter the deadly Cave of Wonders to retrieve a magic lamp.

Aladdin finds the lamp and becomes the master of the genie who gives him three wishes. His first wish is to become Prince Ali in order to win Jasmine. She recognizes him, as does Jafar, who throws him into the ocean. Using his second wish, Aladdin is saved.

Jafar and his parrot, Iago, steal the lamp and send Aladdin to a frozen wasteland. Jafar becomes the sultan and the most powerful sorcerer in the world. Aladdin returns and tricks Jafar into using his final wish to become a genie himself and is trapped in the lamp. Using his own last wish, Aladdin frees the original genie. The sultan changes the law so that Jasmine can marry a commoner like Aladdin rather than a prince.

Behind the Animation

- The peddler who introduces the movie and is voiced by Robin Williams was originally intended to be revealed as the genie at the end. Williams improvised 16 hours of material in his recording sessions.

- *Aladdin* was the first animated film to gross more than $200 million domestically in its initial theatrical release. Worldwide, it grossed over $500 million in its first run.

- Aladdin was originally going to be 13 years old and resemble actor Michael J. Fox, but was changed to being 18 and looking more like actor Tom Cruise so that it would be more convincing to have him as a romantic leading character.

- Comedians John Candy, Steve Martin, John Goodman, Martin Short, Matt Frewer, and Eddie Murphy were all considered at some point to do the voice of the genie, but the directors said the part was always written specifically for Robin Williams.

- The lyrics for the opening song, "Arabian Nights", were changed in July 1993 from "Where they cut off your ear if they don't like your face" in the original release to "Where it's flat and immense and the heat is intense". The change first appeared on the 1993 video release and all subsequent theatrical re-releases.

Quotable Quotes

You're only in trouble if you get caught.
— Aladdin

....

All right, Sparky, here's the deal. If you wanna court the little lady, you gotta be a straight shooter. Do you got it? Tell her the truth!
— Genie

....

To be my own master. Such a thing would be greater than all the magic and all the treasures in all the world.
— Genie

....

Like so many things, it is not what is outside, but what is inside that counts. This is no ordinary lamp. It once changed the course of a young man's life. A young man who, like this lamp, was more than what he seemed. A diamond in the rough.
— Merchant

The Lion King (1994)

On Pride Rock in Africa, the birth of Simba to lion ruler Mufasa is cause for celebration from all the animals. The young cub is filled with mischief and an urge for adventure. His father tries to teach him the values and responsibilities he'll need when he becomes king.

A jealous uncle named Scar wants to remove Simba and ascend the throne himself. Allying himself with three outcast hyenas, Scar orchestrates the death of Mufasa when the latter tries to save Simba from a wildebeest stampede.

Feeling responsible, Simba runs off into the jungle and forges a friendship with meerkat Timon and warthog Pumbaa, and embraces a "no worries" philosophy.

Scar's rule has resulted in the Pride Lands becoming a wasteland with no food or water. Nala, Simba's female childhood friend, tracks him down and urges him to return to take his rightful place. Guided by his father's mandrill friend and advisor, Rafiki, Simba is inspired to do so.

Simba confronts Scar and learns the truth of his father's death. During a fierce battle, Simba tosses Scar off Pride Rock where he is attacked by the hyenas. Simba becomes the new lion king, marries Nala, and has a son.

Behind the Animation

- The two-and-a-half minute wildebeest stampede took almost three years to animate. A brand-new computer program had to be written that allowed hundreds of animals to run in random paths without colliding into each other.

- Disney has always claimed the story and characters were not inspired by Osamu Tezuka's *Kimba the White Lion*. During production the film was known as "Bamlet", since the pitch was "Bambi in Africa" meets "Hamlet".

- Until the release of *Frozen* (2013), this film was the highest grossing animated feature of all time. The soundtrack is also the number one most purchased soundtrack for animated films so far.

- Many members of the production crew spent time at Hell's Gate National Park in Kenya for inspiration on the Pride Lands and how lions lived. They recall tying a rope behind their Land Rover and driving slowly as lion cubs chased the rope, batting and playing with it just like house cats.

- Comedians Cheech Marin and Tommy Chong were going to voice two of the hyenas, but Chong was unavailable. One hyena researcher sued Disney for defamation of character of the animals, and another who had helped animators observe captive hyenas urged a boycott of the film.

Quotable Quotes

Everything you see exists together in a delicate balance. As king, you need to understand that balance and respect all the creatures, from the crawling ant to the leaping antelope.
-Mufasa

The past can hurt. But the way I see it, you can either run from it or learn from it.
— Rafiki

You are more than what you have become.
— Mufasa

I'm only brave when I have to be, Simba. Being brave doesn't mean you go looking for trouble.
— Mufasa

Pocahontas (1995)

In 1607, British settlers arrive in the "New World" of America and establish the colony of Jamestown. These men include heroic explorer Captain John Smith and the commander of the group, Governor Ratcliffe, who is obsessed with finding huge amounts of gold. He becomes incensed when none is found.

Chief Powhatan and his free-spirited young daughter, Pocahontas, at first try their best to avoid these intruders, but find themselves involved.

Smith, who represents progress, and Pocahontas, who advocates for respect of the Earth, develop a relationship, and with Grandmother Willow discuss bringing a peace between their two groups. This hope is shattered when Pocahontas' suitor, the warrior Kocoum, is killed by a British sailor, sparking a war.

When Smith is sentenced to execution, Pocahontas throws herself between her father and Smith, begging for a cessation of all hostilities. Her father relents. Smith repays his kind gesture by jumping in front of the chief and taking the bullet shot by Ratcliffe, who is arrested by the crew. Smith returns to England for medical treatment and to testify against Ratcliffe, while Pocahontas remains with her tribe.

Behind the Animation

- Pocahontas gives the wounded John Smith some willow bark to help ease the pain. Willow bark contains salicylic acid, the basis of aspirin.

- Co-director Mike Gabriel had a hand-made poster consisting of a drawing of Tiger Lily from *Peter Pan* (1953) surrounded by forest animals and pitched it to Disney as the story of a girl trapped between the love of her father's people and their enemy.

- Originally, Pocahontas' animal friend was to have been a talking turkey named Redfeather, who thought he was quite a ladies' man and who would be voiced by comedian John Candy. With Candy's death in 1994, and further development on the script, it was determined that no animals should talk.

- Actor David Odgen Stiers provides the voice for both Governor Ratcliffe as well as Ratcliffe's assistant, Wiggins. His other Disney voice credits include the clock Cogsworth in *Beauty and the Beast* (1991) and the arch deacon in *Hunchback of Notre Dame* (1996).

- Shirley "Little Dove" Custalow-McGowan was a descendent of the Powhatan Indians and consulted with the Disney Studio three times about the film, but eventually felt that the production was not adhering strictly enough to historical accuracy.

Quotable Quotes

Sometimes the right path is not the easiest one.
— Grandmother Willow

Listen with your heart. You will understand.
— Grandmother Willow

You must choose your own path.
— Powhatan

You think I'm an ignorant savage and you've been so many places, I guess it must be so. But still I cannot see if the savage one is me, how can there be so much that you don't know?
— Pocahontas

The Hunchback of Notre Dame (1996)

Inspired by the Victor Hugo story, Quasimodo is raised by Judge Frollo who confines the hunchback in the bell tower of Paris' Notre Dame Cathedral and verbally abuses him. Quasimodo's friends are the three stone gargoyles who talk only to him.

Frollo hates the city's undesirable gypsy population and plans to eliminate them. However, gypsy dancer Esmeralda makes an impression on Frollo, Quasimodo, and Frollo's captain of the guard, Phoebus. She takes sanctuary in the cathedral and befriends Quasimodo. Frollo attempts to lure her out and find the Court of Miracles where the gypsies hide by convincing Quasimodo he already knows the location and intends to attack it at dawn.

Following Quasimodo, Frollo captures the gypsies and intends to burn Esmeralda at the stake as a witch. Quasimodo rescues her and takes her to the cathedral, while Phoebus releases the gypsies and rallies the citizens of Paris against Frollo and his men who are attempting to break in to the sacred sanctuary.

A battle between Frollo and Quasimodo results in Frollo falling to his death while Quasimodo is saved by Phoebus. Quasimodo accepts that Phoebus and Esmeralda are in love and is hailed by the city as a hero for his heroic actions.

Behind the Animation

- During the song "Out There", the camera pans to a square in the city of Paris where Belle from *Beauty and the Beast* (1991) is seen walking and reading her book, Pumba from *The Lion King* (1994) is being carried on a pole by two men, and another man is shaking out the carpet from *Aladdin* (1992).

- Several animators, including Glen Keane, had office space at the newly opened Disneyland Paris while studying the Notre Dame Cathedral. He said he would often go up to the bell tower to think and draw just as dawn was breaking.

- Originally, the gargoyles were going to be named Chaney, Laughton, and Quinn after three actors who had played Quasimodo in other films: Lon Chaney, Charles Laughton, and Anthony Quinn.

- For the scene where Judge Frollo sings "Hellfire" and sees Esmeralda's image dancing in the flames before him, the Motion Picture Association of America insisted that the Disney animators make Esmeralda's clothing more clearly defined, as she appeared to be nude.

- The Latin chants heard throughout the movie are adapted from actual Gregorian chants, including the "Dies Irae". A portion of the "Dies Irae" music can be heard in the scene where Frollo kills Quasimodo's mother.

Quotable Quotes

Life's not a spectator sport. If watchin' is all you're gonna do, then you're gonna watch your life go by without ya.

— Laverne

•••

All my life, you have told me that the world is a dark, cruel place. But now I see that the only thing dark and cruel about it is people like you.

— Quasimodo

•••

You've chosen a magnificent prison, but it is a prison nonetheless.

— Frollo

•••

What makes a monster and what makes a man?

— Clopin

Hercules (1997)

Occasionally narrated by a Greek chorus of five Muses, the film recounts the story of Hercules, son of Zeus, who stands in the way of Hades taking over Olympus. Hades' minions, Pain and Panic, kidnap and drain much of baby Hercules' great strength and he grows up on Earth as a normal human being.

Learning of his birthright, Hercules partners with his flying horse, Pegasus, and a satyr named Phil to train him to become a great hero. Hades intends to release the Titans to conquer Zeus and Olympus, but the Fates tell him that Hercules still could stop his plan. Hades sends the seductive Megara to trick Hercules in exchange for her freedom.

Hercules falls in love with Meg and agrees to lose his strength for 24 hours to save her from harm. During that day Hades unleashes the destructive Titans, but a normal Hercules continues to battle and regains his strength when Meg sacrifices her life for him. Defeating the Titans, Hercules bargains to rescue Meg's soul and in the process regains all his godhood and defeats Hades. Although offered a place in Olympus by his father, Hercules decides to stay on Earth with Meg.

Behind the Animation

- Hercules is actually the Roman name for the character. The Greek name is Heracles. All of the other mythological characters are referred to by their Greek names. Interestingly, the numbers displayed in the film are Roman numerals.

- John Lithgow originally was cast and spent nine months recording all of the dialog for Hades, but was replaced by James Woods who ad-libbed many of his lines. Jack Nicholson was originally approached to do the role.

- In Greek mythology, there were nine Muses. The five in the film are Calliope (epic poetry), Clio (history), Melpomene (tragedy), Terpsichore (dance), and Thalia (comedy). Early in production, Disney had wanted the Spice Girls musical group to perform the roles.

- The lion skin briefly worn by Hercules is a reference to his first legendary labor of killing the Nemean Lion. The skin looks exactly like Scar from *The Lion King* (1994) and this was done intentionally. Scar's animator, Andreas Deja, was also the main animator for Hercules.

- The hydra was computer-generated rather than hand-drawn because of the difficulty of drawing all those heads individually. Even then, 24,000 separate animation controls were needed to coordinate its thirty heads.

Quotable Quotes

A true hero isn't measured by the size of his strength, but by the strength of his heart.
— Zeus

We dance. We kiss. We schmooze. We carry on. We go home happy. What do you say? Come on.
— Hades

Sometimes it's better to be alone. Nobody can hurt you.
— Meg

People do crazy things...when they're in love.
— Meg

Mulan (1998)

Based on an ancient Chinese poem, the story is about a young woman who takes the place of her aged father when he is required to rejoin the army to defend against the invasion of the Huns. Fa Mulan disguises herself as a man and is advised in her adventures by a small talking dragon named Mushu, who claims he has been assigned by the Fa family spiritual guardians.

She proves herself even more skilled and courageous than her fellow male soldiers. Thanks to her ingenuity, she buries the Hun army with an avalanche in the snow-covered mountains, but is wounded in the process. As the wound is being treated, Mulan is revealed to be a woman and abandoned by her compatriots. She discovers that some of the Huns have survived and plan to capture the emperor in the Imperial City.

With the help from four of her fellow comrades-in-arms and Mushu, Mulan defeats the Huns and rescues the emperor. She is rewarded by the emperor and offered the role of advisor, but decides to return home to her family.

Behind the Animation

- When Mulan sings "Reflection" in her father's shrine, the writings on the temple stones are the names of the Disney animators who worked on the film written in ancient Chinese.

- *Mulan* was the first animated feature done primarily by the Disney Feature Animation Florida studio that had previously done sequences for other films as well as two of the Roger Rabbit cartoon shorts.

- In the summer of 1994, several members of the production team spent three weeks in China gathering information and sketching. The animators also utilized the China Pavilion at Epcot because of its architectural authenticity.

- Songwriter Stephen Schwartz was originally going to write the music and lyrics for the film, but left the production to work on Dreamworks' animated feature, *The Prince of Egypt* (1998).

- Lea Salonga, who does the singing voice for Mulan, also supplied the singing voice for Princess Jasmine in *Aladdin* (1992).

Quotable Quotes

The flower that blooms in adversity is the most rare and beautiful of all.
— The Emperor of China

A single grain of rice can tip the scale. One man may be the difference between victory and defeat.
— The Emperor of China

Why is my reflection someone I don't know? Somehow I cannot hide who I am, though I've tried. When will my reflection show who I am inside?
— Mulan

No matter how the wind howls, the mountain cannot bow to it.
— The Emperor of China

Tarzan (1999)

Based on the popular series of stories by Edgar Rice Burroughs about a young orphaned English boy raised by apes in the African jungle, the character of Tarzan had previously appeared in many popular media adaptations, but never animation.

This version has Tarzan as a young man killing the leopardess who murdered his parents and slowly gaining the respect of his surrogate gorilla father, Kerchak. He becomes friends with the young ape Terk and an elephant named Tantor. A group of English explorers arrive in the jungle. Despite Kerchak's warnings, Tarzan rescues Jane Porter from baboons and bonds with the others as he discovers his human heritage.

Reluctantly, Tarzan leads the curious newcomers to the gorillas and Kerchak threatens to kill them, forcing Tarzan to leave the only family he has ever known. The guide for the party is Clayton, who is actually a poacher and teamed with pirates to capture the gorillas. Tarzan and his friends rush to the rescue, but not before Kerchak is mortally wounded by Clayton. Clayton's battle with Tarzan ends in the poacher's death. Before he dies, Kerchak proclaims Tarzan the new leader of the gorillas.

Professor Porter and his daughter Jane decide to stay with Tarzan in the jungle.

Behind the Animation

- The iconic "Tarzan yell" was performed by actor Brian Blessed, who also did the voice of the villainous hunter Clayton. Animator Randy Haycock used classic movie star Clark Gable as an inspiration for Clayton's appearance.

- *Tarzan* was the first Disney animated film to use "Deep Canvas", a technology developed by Disney to have 2D characters blend in a 3D environment that looks like a painting. The Academy of Motion Picture Arts and Sciences awarded the creators of the process a Technical Achievement Award in 2003.

- Animator Glen Keane's son was extremely interested in skateboarding, so some of the movements of Tarzan in the trees were inspired by skateboarder Tony Hawk.

- Glen Keane thought Tarzan would be easy to animate because he wouldn't have to worry about drawing all the folds, drapery, and shadows on clothes, but it turned out to be even more challenging to capture accurate human musculature. A professor of anatomy would superimpose drawings of correct muscles over the animations so Keane could make corrections.

- Of all the Disney animated features, Tarzan has more deaths of primary or major secondary characters: Kala and Kerchak's first son, Tarzan's English parents, Sabor the leopardess, Kerchak, and Clayton.

Quotable Quotes

There are no trails through a woman's heart.
— Clayton

•••

Close your eyes. Now forget what you see. What do you feel?
— Kala

•••

It can't get any worse, can it? Obviously, it can.
— Jane Porter

•••

Tarzan: "No matter where I go, you will always be my mother."

Kala: "And you will always be in my heart."

Fantasia 2000 (1999)

Following the pattern of the earlier *Fantasia* (1940) animated feature, this film is comprised of eight separate animated segments interpreting musical selections and introduced by different celebrity hosts.

"The Sorcerer's Apprentice" is reused from the original film. The new segments include: Ludwig van Beethoven's "Symphony No. 5", using abstract patterns that resemble butterflies; Ottorino Respighi's "Pines of Rome", with a family of flying humpback whales in the Arctic who rescue a calf trapped in an iceberg; and George Gershwin's "Rhapsody in Blue", about intertwining stories of four New York city residents with artwork in the style of Al Hirschfeld.

In addition, the film features Hans Christian Andersen's "The Steadfast Tin Soldier", the story of a broken toy soldier with only one leg who is in love with a toy ballerina and protects her from a jack-in-the-box with evil designs, set to Dmitri Shostakovich's "Piano Concerto No. 2, Allegro, Opus 102"; Camille Saint-Saëns' "Carnival of the Animals, Finale", with an oddball flamingo fascinated with playing with his yo-yo; Edward Elgar's "Pomp and Circumstance, Marches #1, 2, 3 & 4", starring Donald Duck and his frustrations as an assistant on Noah's Ark; and Igor Stravinsky's "Firebird Suite—1919 Version", portraying the death and rebirth of a forest after volcanic destruction.

Behind the Animation

- The "Rhapsody in Blue" sequence was drawn in the style of caricaturist Al Hirschfeld, who always incorporated the name of his daughter, Nina, into his drawings. There are three "Nina's" in this animated segment: one on the end of Duke's toothpaste tube, one in the fur collar of John's wife, and one in her hair.

- *Fantasia 2000* was the first animated feature film to be presented in IMAX. In Los Angeles, the Disney Company built a temporary IMAX theater to show the film for its first four months of release.

- The bespectacled character of Flying John in the "Rhapsody in Blue" segment was based on animation historian John Culhane, who also served as the inspiration for the character of Mr. Snoops in *The Rescuers* (1977).

- In 1970, the Disney Studio toyed with the idea of making *Musicana*, which would have used musical compositions from different countries as a springboard to explore those particular cultures, as a sort of sequel to *Fantasia* (1940).

- The flamingos in "The Carnival of the Animals" segment were completely animated by Eric Goldberg and were originally supposed to be ostriches like the ones in the original film. The idea was conceived by storyman Joe Grant who had worked on the earlier *Fantasia*.

Quotable Quotes

That age old question: what would happen if you gave a yo-yo to a flock of flamingos?
— James Earl Jones

Walt Disney described the art of animation as a voyage of discovery, into the realms of color, sound, and motion.
— Angela Lansbury

Some (great ideas) made it to the big screen this time, but others—lots of others—how can I put this politely?—didn't.

Bette Midler

All stage magic is a fraud...a hoax...a sham. It's all based on deception and, yes, lying. All of it.
— Penn Jillette

Dinosaur (2000)

The film is an intriguing hybrid of computer-animated characters superimposed over live-action backgrounds. An iguanodon called Aladar is raised by two lemurs in a dangerous prehistoric jungle. Their world is shattered by fiery meteor explosions.

Aladar and some of the surviving lemurs join a multi-species caravan of dinosaurs journeying across a vast wasteland to find a new home in a valley supposedly untouched by the destruction. They are led by the brutal iguanodons Kron and Bruton, who are solely focused on getting to the valley whatever the costs.

A pair of Carnotaurus stalk the group and so Kron abandons some of the weaker members who find refuge in a cave and eventually kill one of the Carnotaurus. The cave leads them to the new land and they see that the other entrance has been blocked by a landslide.

Aladar returns to alert Kron and his group of an alternate entrance, and they are attacked by the remaining Carnotaurus who mortally wounds Kron. Aladar defeats the dinosaur and leads the rest to the valley, where he mates with Kron's sister to birth a new generation of dinosaurs.

Behind the Animation

- The backgrounds were filmed in Canaima National Park and Angel Falls in Venezuela, as well as locations in Hawaii and Tahiti.

- Originally, the film was to be made with no dialog at all, to set it apart from the animated feature film *The Land Before Time* (1988), but CEO Michael Eisner insisted on having the dinosaurs talk.

- When it comes to dinosaurs, the film is a fantasy since it shows many of them together who did not live during the same time period or even at the same physical location. Lemurs appeared millions of years after the dinosaurs, but the directors felt they would be cute.

- Paleontology experts were consulted, as was author and artist James Gurney who was well known for his Dinotopia books. Famed dinosaur illustrator William Stout was a key designer on the film, doing most of his work at home and coming in to the studio every Friday to deliver his artwork.

- For the production of this film and its digital effects, the award-winning Dream Quest Images merged with Disney's in-house computer graphics unit to form a new entity called The Secret Lab. It was dissolved in 2001 when it was determined it would be more cost-effective to outsource the work.

Quotable Quotes

Some things start out big, and some things start out small, very small. But sometimes the smallest thing can make the biggest changes of all.

— Plio

Only if you give up, Bruton. It's your choice, not your fate.

— Plio

Our journey's not over. We can only hope that in some small way our time here will be remembered.

— Plio

You're never going to forget this day, so make it one to remember.

— Plio

The Emperor's New Groove (2000)

During the Incan Empire, a spoiled young emperor named Kuzco gets whatever he wants. He currently wants to build a summer home on a scenic hilltop where llama herder Pacha and his family live, and ignores the peasant's pleas to change his mind.

Kuzco fires aging advisor Yzma who is so embittered that she plots to poison him, but a mistake by her henchman, Kronk, leaves the emperor as a talking llama instead. Yzma takes over the throne for the missing monarch. Pacha offers to help the transformed Kuzco in exchange for saving his home. Yzma and Kronk stalk the pair, who are constantly confronted by perils like cliffs, waterfalls, and crocodiles. They separate when Pacha learns Kuzco lied.

Discovering the truth that Yzma is trying to kill him, Kuzco once again engages the help of Pacha to race to the palace for a cure. Yzma and Kronk beat the pair back to the location and order the guards to kill the llama. After several comedic transformations from the vials in Yzma's secret laboratory, Kuzco regains his human form and throne, and decides to build his summer home on a neighboring hilltop to Pacha's home.

Behind the Animation

- The film was originally to be an epic serious musical entitled *The Kingdom of the Sun*, a retelling of Mark Twain's novel *The Prince and the Pauper* set during the Incan Empire.

- Singer Eartha Kitt supplied the voice for Yzma who is changed into a kitten at the end of the film. Kitt played the role of Catwoman in the third season of the 1966 *Batman* TV series.

- Voice actor Patrick Warburton improvised Kronk's theme song that he hums while his character takes Kuzco (in llama form) to the waterfall in a sack. Disney's Legal Department made Warburton sign over all rights to the improvised song.

- Both Elton John and Phil Collins, who had provided songs for previous Disney animated features, encouraged their friend Sting to work for the studio. Unfortunately, when the film was heavily re-written, most of Sting's work was eliminated because it did not reflect the changes.

- A scene showing Kuzco's guards training for the destruction of Pacha's village was fully animated, scored, and in color when it was deleted from the film. Some of the animation of the guards from this sequence was later used in the final battle.

Quotable Quotes

He's not as dead as we would have hoped.

— Kronk

· ·

When will you learn that all my ideas are good ones?

— Kuzco

· ·

Well, I threw off the emperor's groove. His groove! The rhythm in which he lives his life. His pattern of behavior. I threw it off. And the emperor had me thrown out the window. Don't throw off his groove!

— Old Man

· ·

That is the last time we take directions from a squirrel.

— Yzma

Atlantis: The Lost Empire (2001)

Milo Thatch, who has devoted his life to finding the lost city of Atlantis, is funded by a millionaire to head an expedition using an old journal as a guide. The skilled experts that have been assembled are led by Commander Rourke, who guides the submarine *Ulysses* through many underwater perils until they reach their destination.

The city of Atlantis, located in a network of underground tunnels, has been protected for 9000 years by a dome that covers it and is powered by the mystic crystal known as the Heart of Atlantis.

An ancient race still lives in the city. Milo discovers that his crew are actually mercenaries who intend to steal the crystal. Sensing a threat, the crystal merges with Princess Kida who is taken hostage by Rourke after he mortally wounds the king. Milo convinces most of the crew not to proceed with their plans.

Milo battles Rourke, turning him into crystal, and as a volcano erupts, Kida uses the power of the crystal to create a protective shield to save the city. The mercenaries return home swearing never to reveal the secret while Milo stays with Kida.

Behind the Animation

- Marc Okrand, who created the Altantean language for this film, also created the Vulcan, Romulan, and Klingon languages for the original *Star Trek* movies.

- Actor Jim ("Hey, Vern! It's me, Ernest!") Varney, who did the voice for character "Cookie" Farnsworth, died of lung cancer in February 2000 before *Atlantis* was finished; the film is dedicated to him. The dialog of the Farnsworth character in the final scene was provided by Steve Barr.

- A proposed animated television series entitled *Team Atlantis* was planned, but the weak performance of the film resulted in it being cancelled. Three episodes from the aborted series were combined in a direct-to-video 2003 sequel called *Atlantis: Milo's Return*.

- At one point, so many animators, technicians, and other artists were laboring on the film that work was being done by all three of the Disney Feature Animation studios in existence at the time.

- Originally, *Atlantis* was to be an action-adventure film in the style of the classic Ray Harryhausen fantasy movies and Disney's *20,000 Leagues Under the Sea* (1954), and would have included battles with squid bats, lava whales, and bugs the size of trucks.

Quotable Quotes

We done a lot of things we're not proud of. Robbing graves, eh, plundering tombs, double parking. But, nobody got hurt. Well, maybe somebody got hurt, but nobody we knew.

— Vinny

....

What they have to teach us, we have already learned.

— King Kashekim Nedakh

....

I didn't say it was the smart thing, but it is the right thing.

— Milo

....

We are not thriving. True, our people live, but our culture is dying. We are like a stone the ocean beats against. With each passing year a little more of us is worn away.

— Princess Kida

Lilo and Stitch (2002)

Somewhere in the galaxy, evil genius scientist Jumba is sentenced to prison for the illegal creation of Experiment 626, a destructive little blue multi-limbed monster who escapes his sentenced exile to a desert asteroid and ends up on the Hawaiian island of Kauai.

An unusual native girl named Lilo adopts him, thinking he is just an odd looking dog, and names him Stitch. Her older sister, Nani, has quite a challenge caring for over-dramatic little Lilo, since they are both recently orphaned and a social worker wants to sends Lilo to a foster home.

The Galactic Federation sends Jumba and a guide named Pleakley to recapture the indestructible Stitch. Their failed attempts cause more trouble for the family, forcing Stitch to leave.

Captain Gantu, newly assigned to the recapture task by the Federation, nabs both Stitch and Lilo, but Stitch escapes. He must rally Jumba, Pleakley, and Nani to give chase in a spaceship to rescue Lilo from Gantu. After doing so, the Grand Councilwoman appears and dismisses Gantu. She assigns Stitch to serve his exile on Earth with Lilo and Nani. Jumba and Pleakley decide to stay as well.

Behind the Animation

- The original (completely animated) finale had Stitch and Jumba hijacking an airplane to chase Gantu and crashing into buildings. After the terrorist attack on September 11, 2001, it was re-animated using another spaceship and taking place in unpopulated areas.

- The story was originally set in Kansas, where Stitch's spaceship would have crashed. Co-writer Chris Sanders felt that the isolated area would limit the amount of damage that Stitch could do. Stitch would live in the forest and interact with mild-mannered animals.

- Chris Sanders was the co-director, co-writer, co-character designer, and the voice of Stitch, a character he had created in 1985 for a children's book never published.

- All the license plates in the film read "A113", including Cobra Bubbles' rental car, Captain Gantu's spaceship, Nani's car, a fire truck, a tanker truck, and a license plate in Lilo's room. The number is a reference to a room at California Institute of the Arts where many of the artists studied character animation.

- Sanders decorated the studio with Hawaiian-style props like tiki torches and surfboards. The production team spent weeks in Hawaii, studying things like the quality of light falling from the sky and the way vegetation blooms thickly around isolated island communities.

Quotable Quotes

Ohana means family, family means nobody gets left behind. Or forgotten.
— Lilo

What must it be like to have nothing, not even memories to look back on in the middle of the night?
— Jumba

It seems clear to me that you need her a lot more than she needs you.
— Mr. Cobra Bubbles

This is your badness level. It's unusually high for someone your size. We have to fix that.
— Lilo

Treasure Planet (2002)

Inspired by the classic Robert Louis Stevenson novel *Treasure Island*, the story is set in the future where space travel is common. A troubled teenager named Jim Hawkins, who enjoys solar surfing, worries his single mother, the owner of a local inn.

A dying pirate gives Jim a map to the planet where the space pirate Flint buried his great treasure. Reluctantly, Jim's mother allows him to accompany Dr. Doppler and Captain Amelia to find the legendary loot. On board is the ship's cook Long John Silver, a cyborg who plans to lead a mutiny once they get there.

Jim and Silver bond while Jim is troubled by an incident aboard ship where the first mate was lost. When they reach their destination, the crew does indeed mutiny and Doppler, Amelia, and Jim escape and meet B.E.N., a robot who has lost most of his memory. They are all eventually captured by Silver and his crew, and Jim is forced to use the map to reveal a portal that can be opened anywhere in the universe.

The portal can access the inside of a planet-sized space station filled with treasure. However, the area is set to explode if it is discovered. Thanks to Jim's ingenuity and courage, they are able to escape and return to their home spaceport.

Behind the Animation

- The name of the spaceship, the RLS *Legacy*, is an homage to Robert Louis Stevenson.

- *Treasure Planet* was originally called *Treasure Island in Space*. It was pitched to Disney by co-directors Ron Clements and John Musker three times over the years. Finally, Musker and Clements only agreed to direct *Hercules* (1997) if they could make this film.

- The artists designing the film operated on a rule they called the "70/30 Law", which meant that the overall look of the film's artwork should be 70% traditional and 30% sci-fi. The same rule was applied for the sound effects and music.

- Feeling that bulky space suits and helmets would take all the romance out of the story and make it challenging to show emotion and movement, the concept of "etherium" was created so that it was an outer space filled with atmosphere.

- After supervising the work on the character of Long John Silver, who was a combination of hand-drawn and CGI elements, animator Glen Keane strongly considered leaving the Disney Studio because he didn't feel he was being challenged. He remained when Disney offered him the chance to direct his own personal project, a dark retelling of the story of Rapunzel.

Quotable Quotes

You got the makings of greatness in you, but you got to take the helm and chart your own course. Stick to it, no matter the squalls! And when the time comes you get the chance to really test the cut of your sails, and show what you're made of.

— John Silver

You give up a few things, chasing a dream.

— John Silver

I've lost my mind! You haven't found it, have you?

— B.E.N.

I speaks nothin' but me heart, at all times.

— John Silver

Brother Bear (2003)

In post-Ice Age North America, three brothers gather as the youngest one named Kenai is given his spiritual totem of a bear. Kenai is not fond of bears, especially after his oldest brother dies in an encounter with one. Kenai kills the bear and is transformed into a bear himself. His other brother vows to kill the bear that seemingly killed his younger brother.

Kenai reluctantly agrees to accompany Koda, a young cub whose mother has gone missing, to a salmon run to reunite the pair, and also in hopes of reaching a sacred spot in the mountains where he can be turned back into human form.

A pair of Canadian moose occasionally pop up in the wilderness to lighten the dark tale where the angry middle brother continues to hunt Kenai and Koda. When the bears finally reach the salmon run, Koda tells a story and Kenai realizes that when he was in human form he killed Koda's mother. He reveals the truth to the horrified cub.

Later saving Koda's life from his middle brother's wrath, Kenai is transformed back into a human, but asks to remain as a bear to care for Koda.

Behind the Animation

- *Brother Bear* was the last animated feature film produced at Disney Feature Animation Florida. The studio was shut down shortly after its release.

- While for the most part traditionally animated, some scenes like the salmon run and caribou stampede utilized computer-generated artwork. The artists did life-drawing sessions with live bear cubs, and were also taken to the nearby Fort Wilderness Resort and Campground at Walt Disney World for drawing sessions three times a week for two months.

- The two goofy bull moose, Tuke and Rutt, were voiced by comedians Rick Moranis and Dave Thomas, who had created the characters of Canadian brothers Bob and Doug MacKenzie for the sketch comedy show *SCTV* in 1980. They used those same personas for the moose.

- After Kenai is transformed into a bear, the film shifts from a 1.75:1 aspect ratio to the CinemaScope ratio of 2.35:1 to give the audience a sense of seeing the world differently. Phil Collins wrote a "transformation song" that was translated into Inuit and then sung by a full Bulgarian choir. It was cut from the film.

- The background and layout artists studied the work of landscape artist Albert Bierstadt, a favorite of then Disney CEO Michael Eisner.

Quotable Quotes

Everything will become clear to you when you see things through another's eyes.
— Kenai's spirit voices

Let love guide your actions, and one day, you'll be a man.
— Tanana

Never try to milk a caribou.
— Kenai

My eyes were watering, and my tongue was swollen, and from that moment on, I was more careful about what I licked!
— Koda

Home on the Range (2004)

The widow Pearl owns the small farm called Patch of Heaven and learns that she only has three days to raise $750 to pay back the bank or they will take her land. Her three cows, Maggie, Grace, and Mrs. Calloway, go to town hoping to win prize money at the local fair.

Cattle rustler Alameda Slim has been mysteriously stealing cattle, and an unscrupulous bounty hunter named Rico aims to collect the $750 reward on the bandit.

The cows decide to catch the villain themselves by hiding in a large herd that will tempt Slim, who appears and does a yodel that puts the animals in a trance. As he is leading them away, the three cows come to their senses at the last moment.

The sheriff's horse, Buck, vows to capture Slim to prove his worth, and the lady cows hook up with a peg-legged rabbit named Lucky Jack who leads them to Slim's hideout. He reveals that he steals the cattle to drive ranchers into debt so he can easily buy their land using his ill-gotten gains from cattle rustling.

The cows are able to expose Slim and use the reward money to save Patch of Heaven.

Behind the Animation

- The film earned its "PG" rating primarily due to Maggie's remark about her large udders: "Yeah, they're real. Quit staring."

- Because of its extremely poor performance at the box office, this film ushered in a five-year hiatus of Disney making traditional hand-drawn animated features until *The Princess and the Frog* (2009). The film made back less than half its cost during its first run.

- *Home on the Range* was originally going to be a supernatural adventure called *Sweating Bullets* with a calf named "Bullets" saving his herd from a band of ghostly cattle rustlers who were killing cattle in revenge for having been trampled to death.

- Alameda Slim was named after Montana Silm (Wilf Carter), a popular Canadian country music singer and yodeler. Alameda's hypnotic yodeling was inspired by the classic tale of the Pied Piper. The yodeling was done by Randy Quaid.

- This film was the final Disney animated feature to use the CAPS (Computer Animation Production System) to color the artwork. After *Home on the Range*, it was dismantled since no more hand-drawn animated films were planned.

Quotable Quotes

Now, let's not play the shame-and-blame game. This is an organic problem, and there's a holistic solution.

— Grace

··

All right, what part of "cover me" didn't we understand?

— Maggie

··

Step lightly, girls! The male of the species can be extremely hostile.

— Mrs. Calloway

··

You wanna get nuts? Let's get nuts!

— Audrey

Chicken Little (2005)

The fable of a small chicken who is struck by an acorn and misinterprets it as the sky falling is expanded in this film to the chicken being a middle school boy who experienced a similar incident and provoked a panic in his hometown of Oakey Oaks and is still trying to live down his blunder.

A year later, he tries to redeem himself by joining the baseball team and his game-winning home run seems to have put him on that path, especially in the eyes of his single father. However, Little is struck on the head again by a hexagonal chameleon-color changing piece, but this time enlists the aid of his eccentric outcast schoolmates to investigate this extraterrestrial mystery.

The piece is part of an alien spaceship hovering over the town in disguise. When he alerts the town, the aliens disappear leaving an orange alien child behind.

Little is ridiculed again until the aliens return with more spaceships to retrieve the child and start vaporizing the town and its inhabitants. It is all a misunderstanding and all the vaporizing was actually teleporting things aboard the UFO. With the lost alien child returned, all is restored to normal.

Behind the Animation

- There are 250,000 feathers on Chicken Little. The character was originally going to be a girl. Previously, Disney had adapted the fable as a cartoon short entitled *Chicken Little* in 1943.

- This was the last theatrical film released featuring work by comedian Don Knotts, who voiced Mayor Turkey Lurkey.

- The co-production deal between Disney and Pixar was set to expire at this time. *Chicken Little* was made to determine whether Disney could do a successful CGI film without Pixar, and it was a modest success. On January 24, 2006, Disney announced its intent to purchase Pixar; it completed the purchase on May 5, 2006.

- Abby Mallard was nicknamed "The Ugly Duckling" to imply she would grow up to be a beautiful swan. Jodie Foster, Helen Hunt, and Laura Dern were all considered for the role.

- *Chicken Little* was the last movie to use the name Walt Disney Feature Animation. Starting with *Meet the Robinsons* (2007), future films were produced by the renamed Walt Disney Animation Studios. This is also the last animated feature to use the 1985 Walt Disney Pictures logo.

Quotable Quotes

This excitement isn't just about the fun of baseball. It's not about the prize. It's about the gloating and rubbing their noses in it. The "Nah-Nah-Nah-Nah-Nah! We beat you!" taunting, if you will, that comes with the winning.
— Dog Announcer

You gotta be ready to listen to your children, even if they have nothing to say.
— Buck Cluck

Prepare to hurt, and I don't mean emotionally like I do!
— Chicken Little

I'm not gonna sugarcoat it; I've seen road kill with faster reflexes.
— Dog Announcer

Meet the Robinsons (2007)

Very loosely based on the short children's book by William Joyce, the film focuses on a twelve-year-old orphan named Lewis who is constantly inventing things. His memory scanner invention for the science fair is sabotaged by a mysterious bowler-hat-wearing man. Lewis is contacted by thirteen-year-old Wilbur Robinson from the future who whisks Lewis away in an airborne time machine to the year 2037.

The machine breaks down and Lewis spends time with Wilbur's quirky family. Lewis discovers that Wilbur is actually his son from the future, and the supposedly villainous Bowler Hat Man is actually his roommate at the orphanage.

Apparently, Lewis' constant inventing kept his roommate awake, so he was too tired to make an important catch in a baseball game and that started a series of unfortunate events in his life. He has vowed revenge on the boy inventor, but when he gets it, the future becomes a nightmare dominated by clones of his robotic bowler hat.

Lewis eventually sets things right and the future is bright and happy for everyone.

Behind the Animation

- A photo of Walt Disney is seen in Lewis' room at the 6th Street Orphanage. Another photo is of inventor Nikola Tesla.

- Over a hundred animated feature films were produced the same year. *Shrek the Third*, *Ratatouille*, *The Simpsons Movie*, and *Bee Movie* all earned more than this film, which ended up in fifth place at the box office.

- John Lasseter came on board as chief creative officer for Pixar and Disney during the production of *Meet the Robinsons* and made suggestions for new story elements and action scenes, including a dinosaur chase, a new ending, and an improved villain.

- The dinosaur mascot for the baseball team is based on a character from another book by author William Joyce: *Dinosaur Bob and His Adventures with the Family Lazardo*.

- In 2037, there is an amusement park called "Todayland" that is a tribute to Disneyland's Tomorrowland. Space Mountain and the Rocket Jets can be clearly seen along with the distinctive lettering.

Quotable Quotes

Pop quiz: who have you met, and what have you learned?

— Wilbur

....

Just a little tip for the future, I am always right. Even when I'm wrong, I'm right.

— Franny

....

I'm sorry your life turned out so bad. But don't blame me. You messed it up yourself. You just focused on the bad stuff when all you had to do was let go of the past and keep moving forward...

— Lewis

....

I'M NOT EXAGGERATING! Well, yes I am, but that's not the point!

— Wilbur

Bolt (2008)

Bolt is a white shepherd dog who is the star of a popular action-oriented television series and who believes he actually has genetically enhanced powers. He shares a genuine affection for his young girl co-star, Penny.

Mistakenly believing that Penny has been kidnapped by the villain in the series, Bolt goes to the rescue and winds up in a cardboard box sent to New York City where he assumes the Styrofoam packing has robbed him of his powers. He teams up with an alley cat named Mittens to find his way back to Hollywood. He is also joined by a fan of his television show, a hamster named Rhino who spends most of his time in a plastic exercise ball.

After a series of adventures including being captured by an animal shelter, Bolt realizes he is just a normal dog, but a pep talk from Rhino inspires him to continue.

Just as they arrive at the studio, the stand-in for Bolt panics during a scene and accidentally sets the sound stage on fire with Penny trapped there. Bolt rescues the girl with the help of some firefighters. Penny and her mother adopt Bolt, Mittens, and Rhino, and live happily in a rural home.

Behind the Animation

- The studio lot area where the fictional television series is being filmed resembles the Riverside Drive entrance to the Disney Studio.

- The project was originally developed as *American Dog* by Chris Sanders, co-writer/co-director of *Lilo and Stitch* (2002). When he resisted changes that John Lasseter wanted made, Sanders left Disney to co-write/co-direct Dreamworks' *How to Train Your Dragon* (2010).

- John Lasseter brought his pet chinchilla to an animators' retreat during production and the pet helped inspire the design of Rhino. The crew did adopt a real hamster to study named Doink! that lived at the studio.

- Co-directors Byron Howard and Chris Williams and lighting director Adolph Lusinsky were inspired by the paintings of Edward Hopper, George Bellows, and other Ashcan School Artists from the early 20th century, as well as the works of cinematographers Gordon Willis and Vilmos Zsigmond.

- Art director Paul Felix, director of lighting Adolph Lusinksy, and other members of the production team went on the road to the locations where the characters would visit, including the streets of New York, the San Francisco docks, an Ohio trailer park, Kentucky, and West Virginia, to study how the light in those places interacted with the scenery.

Quotable Quotes

Ring, ring! Who's there? Destiny? I've been expecting your call.

— Rhino

• •

Nothing you think is real is real!

— Mittens

• •

Every minute spent in your company becomes the new greatest minute of my life!

— Rhino

• •

They need a hero, Bolt! Someone who, no matter what the odds, will do what's right. They need a hero to tell them that sometimes the impossible can become possible...if... you're...awesome!

— Rhino

The Princess and The Frog (2009)

In 1926, a young black waitress named Tiana tries to save enough money to open her own restaurant. Her best friend, a rich white Southern belle named Charlotte is excited because Prince Naveen of Maldonia will be attending a ball thrown by her father.

When the prince visits a local voodoo witch doctor named Dr. Facilier, he is transformed into a frog while his man servant is magically disguised as Naveen in order to marry the rich Charlotte so Dr. Facilier can have the fortune.

Mistaking Tiana for a princess at the ball, the frog begs her to kiss him and when she does, she becomes a frog as well. They escape to a bayou where they meet Louis, a trumpet-playing alligator, and Ray, a Cajun firefly in love with the evening star. Voodoo Priestess Madame Odie tells the frogs that Naveen must kiss a real princess for the curse to be broken.

Facilier tempts Tiana to give him back his magical charm in exchange for her restaurant. Tiana destroys the charm and the demons claim Facilier instead.

The two frogs marry, but that makes Tiana a real princess so their kiss transforms them both back to human form and they open a restaurant.

Behind the Animation

- Tiana is left-handed just like actress Anika Noni Rose, who supplies her voice. Rose was in her late 30s when she did the voice of the 19-year-old Tiana. The character is somewhat inspired by the life of Leah Chase, the queen of Creole cuisine, and a black chef in New Orleans.

- While Prohibition was in force until 1933, alcohol is freely served at the party, on the riverboat, and at Tiana's restaurant at the end of the film.

- Animator Eric Goldberg supervised the animation on the Art Deco fantasy sequence of Tiana dreaming of her restaurant, basing it on the art of Harlem Renaissance painter Aaron Douglas.

- Composer Randy Newman, who was born in New Orleans, also provides the voice for the character of Cousin Randy.

- Tiana wears eleven different outfits in the film, including two work outfits, two costumes for the masquerade ball, imaginary clothes at "Tiana's Place", outerwear like her green coat, her wedding dress, and the actual outfit she wears at the real "Tiana's Place".

Quotable Quotes

My daddy never did get what he wanted. But he had what he needed. He had love. He never lost sight o' what was really important.

— Tiana

....

The only thing important is what's UNDER the skin.

— Mama Odie

....

You wish and you dream with all your little heart. But you remember that old star can only take you part of the way. You got to help him with some hard work of your own.

— James

....

The evening star is shinin' bright. So make a wish and hold on tight. There's magic in the air tonight, and anything can happen.

— Tiana

Tangled (2010)

Rapunzel is born with golden hair that has the power to heal. Mother Gothel steals the baby and imprisons her in a tall remote tower, and the restorative hair keeps Gothel young. With only her pet chameleon Pascal and occasional visits by Gothel, the now eighteen-year-old girl has grown restless.

Thief Flynn Rider, who has stolen a royal tiara, stumbles across the tower and is captured by Rapunzel. She bargains to have him take her to see the kingdom.

An incident at a local pub where soldiers are tracking down Rider finds the two trapped in a flooding cave, but rescued by Rapunzel's hair. An uneasy truce is formed with Maximus, one of the horses of the royal guard, and the couple make it to the kingdom in time to enjoy the release of the floating lanterns.

Rider is captured by his old crime partners, but all are arrested. Gothel returns Rapunzel to the tower. Rider is rescued by the patrons of the pub and goes to rescue Rapunzel. However, Gothel mortally stabs him before she herself dies. Rider is healed by a tear from Rapunzel and the two return to the kingdom where they will marry.

Behind the Animation

- Glen Keane worked on developing the film for fourteen years, but left the project in 2009 after having a heart attack. The final film is much different from his original vision.

- Over 45,000 floating sky lanterns are seen in the "I See The Light" sequence that was inspired by the traditional Indonesian ceremonies where people send rice paper lanterns into the sky.

- Disney changed the title of the film from *Rapunzel* because it feared that people might think it was just another princess film for young girls and they wanted it to appeal to a broader audience as a comedic adventure.

- At 18 years old, Rapunzel's never-cut hair is 70 feet (840 inches) long and consists of approximately 100,000 individual strands.

- Actresses Idina Menzel and Kristen Bell both auditioned for the role of Rapunzel. Kristin Chenoweth, Reese Witherspoon, and Natalie Portman did as well.

Quotable Quotes

I promise. And when I promise something, I never, ever, break that promise. Ever.

— Rapunzel

....

You can't tell anyone about this, okay? It could ruin my whole reputation. Well, a fake reputation is all a man has.

— Flynn Rider

....

You were wrong about the world. And you were wrong about me!

— Rapunzel

....

Rapunzel: "What if it's not everything I dreamed it would be?

Flynn Rider: "Well, that's the good part, I guess. You get to go find a new dream."

Winnie the Pooh (2011)

The film is based on three stories found in the A.A. Milne books.

While out searching for honey, Pooh discovers that Eeyore has lost his tail. Christopher Robin holds a contest to see who can find a suitable replacement.

The next day, Pooh goes to visit Christopher and finds a note that Owl misinterprets as news that a monster known as "Backson" has captured the boy. Rabbit sets a trap for the creature, and Tigger tries to teach Eeyore to fight the monster by disguising himself as one.

Accidentally, Pooh falls into the Backson pit followed by Rabbit, Kanga, Roo, Owl, and Eeyore. Piglet is confronted by Tigger in his Backson outfit and tries to escape using a red balloon, but only dislodges some of the storybook letters into the pit.

Piglet and Tigger finally end up in the pit as well, but they all use the letters as a ladder for everyone to escape. Christopher Robin returns and explains that he meant "back soon".

Later, Pooh visits Owl and sees that he is using Eeyore's tail as a bell-pull without realizing what it really is. Pooh returns the tail to Eeyore and Christopher rewards him with a pot of honey.

Behind the Animation

- Except for *The Many Adventures of Winnie the Pooh* (1977) and this film, all the other Winnie the Pooh movies that were released direct-to-video as well as those released theatrically were produced by DisneyToon Studios.

- The Winnie the Pooh stuffed bear in the beginning of the film was made by Sylvia Mattinson, the wife of famed Disney animator and director Burny Mattinson, who was the key storyboard artist for the film. It was originally made for the first feature, but never used.

- Several scenes from the original trailer do not appear in the final film. In fact, the film originally was going to adapt five stories and there would have been a scene featuring all of Rabbit's family.

- Robert Lopez and his wife Kristen Anderson-Lopez composed seven songs for the film and would later write the songs for *Frozen* (2013). Two of the songs were inspired by their experiences with their young daughter, Annie.

- Eric Goldberg, who oversaw the animation for Rabbit in the film, was inspired to draw the character by looking at footage of the late President Nixon, plus imagery of John Cleese's character Basil Fawlty, animator John Lounsbery (one of the Nine Old Men), and some original model sheets provided by veteran animator Burny Mattinson.

Quotable Quotes

Artistic talent runs through my family. In fact, it practically stampedes.
— Owl

It's a good thing I noticed it. Otherwise, I wouldn't have seen it.
— Winnie the Pooh

Take my time. What a wonderful idea!
— Winnie thePooh

Well, I believed you, but my tummy had to check for itself.
— Winnie the Pooh

Wreck-It Ralph (2012)

Wreck-It Ralph is a misunderstood villain in a video game entitled *Fix-It Felix Jr.*, where Felix must repair every apartment building window Ralph breaks. The game's thirtieth anniversary prompts Ralph to attend a support group of depressed video game villains.

Feeling unloved, Ralph does some ill-advised and dangerous game jumping in order to win a medal and become a hero. He visits the violent sci-fi military shooter game *Hero's Duty*, but then ends up in *Sugar Rush*, a game of go-kart racing in a world of candy. Ralph befriends Vanellope von Schweetz and they work together to each get their first taste of victory.

Other arcade characters worry that Ralph's involvement will lead to consequences of the games being put out of commission. King Candy lies to Ralph and gets him to leave after destroying Vanelope's hopes for the big race.

Felix fixes the wrecked kart and in the race it is discovered that King Candy is an imposter and that Cy-bugs from *Hero's Duty* are destroying the game. Ralph comes up with a plan to attract and destroy the menace, and even though there are complications, it all works out in the end, with all the characters happy in their respective games.

Behind the Animation

- Disney created an actual *Fix-It Felix Jr.* arcade game for people to play that was available in Tomorrowland at Disneyland. Before *Wreck-It Ralph*, Disney had unsuccessfully tried over the years to develop two animated feature films based on video game: *High Score* and *Joe Jump*.

- The high score on the *Fix-It Felix Jr.* game cabinet is 120501, a tribute to the birth date of Walt Disney: December 5, 1901.

- The doughnut-shaped police in the *Sugar Rush* game are named Wynnchel and Duncan, a reference to two familiar American doughnut chains: Winchell's Donut House and Dunkin' Donuts.

- There are approximately 188 characters in the film, including some from popular video games like Clyde from *Pac-Man*, Doctor Eggman from *Sonic the Hedgehog*, and Bowser from *Super Mario Bros*, just in the support group alone.

- The animators considered making Ralph look 8-bit the entire time, but it was deemed he wouldn't be lovable enough. The design of Ralph began as an animal dressed as a bum, evolved into a big white gorilla, and only became human about six iterations into the development.

Quotable Quotes

I'm bad, and that's good. I will never be good, and that's not bad. There's no one I'd rather be than me.
— Wreck-It Ralph

I don't need a medal to tell me I'm a good guy.
— Wreck-it Ralph

Labels not make you happy. Good, bad, ngggh-hhhh...you must love you.
— Zombie

I know it's tough, but heroes have to make the tough choices sometimes.
— King Candy

Frozen (2013)

Elsa can manipulate ice and accidentally injures her younger sister, Anna. The trolls are able to heal the girl, but a guilty Elsa locks herself away in her room, cutting off contact with Anna.

The parents die in a storm at sea and Elsa must now ascend the throne. Anna foolishly agrees to marry a young royal she has just met and an upset Elsa unleashes her powers, bringing an eternal winter to the kingdom. Panicking, Elsa flees the castle for the mountains where she creates her own ice palace sanctuary.

Anna follows to mend their relationship, leaving her fiancé in charge. She meets an ice vendor named Kristoff who she convinces to lead her up the mountain where they meet a living snowman named Olaf.

When the sisters do reunite, Elsa once again wounds Anna with her icy powers. Her frozen heart can only be thawed by an act of true love, so Kristoff takes Anna back to her fiancé who has tracked down and captured Elsa and imprisoned her.

His true plan was to seize control of Arendale. Elsa escapes in the blizzard, followed by Anna and Olaf searching for Kristoff. When Anna's fiancé attempts to kill Elsa, Anna sacrifices herself to save her, ending the winter and mending Anna's frozen heart.

Behind the Animation

- There is a brief cameo of Rapunzel with short brown hair and Flynn Rider attending the ceremony when the gates to Arendale are opened.

- A real-life reindeer was brought into the studio for observation. The animal demonstrated an unusual technique for taking care of an itch on its ear. It used his back leg, like a dog, and the movement was incorporated into the film.

- The credits include the disclaimer: "The views and opinions expressed by Kristoff in the film that all men eat their own boogers are solely his own and do not necessarily reflect the views or opinions of the Walt Disney Company or the filmmakers."

- To give the southern California animators a reminder about the physics of snow, the crew was sent to Jackson Hole, Wyoming, for a "snow day", including at one point having both men and women wear a long dress to see how it felt in the snow.

- For the song "Do You Want to Build a Snowman?" three different singers perform: Katie Lopez (daughter of the songwriters) as five-year-old Anna, Agatha Lee Monn (daughter of co-director Jennifer Lee) as tween Anna, and Kristen Bell as eighteen-year-old Anna.

Quotable Quotes

The sky's awake. So I'm awake. So we have to play.

— Anna

Some people are worth melting for. Just... maybe not right this second.

— Olaf

The cold never bothered me anyway.

— Elsa

The heart is not so easily changed, but the head can be persuaded.

— Grand Pabbie

Big Hero 6 (2014)

Hiro Hamada is a 14-year-old robotics genius who lives in the futuristic fictional city of San Fransokyo where he is being raised by his aunt and older brother. Hiro tries to follow in his brother's footsteps by entering his invention of microbots at a science fair. A fire and explosion destroys his creation and kills his brother.

Several weeks later he activates one of his brother's final projects, an inflatable robot built as a medical assistant named Baymax. He discovers that a man in a Kabuki mask is mass producing his microbots, so he enlists his brother's four university friends to track down the mystery. In addition, he builds special armor for Baymax and the group becomes high-tech heroes.

The masked man turns out to be his older brother's university professor who did not die in the explosion, but is using Hiro's technology to seek revenge for the loss of his daughter during a teleportation experiment. He allowed Hiro's brother to die so he could steal the microbots.

There is a big battle where Baymax sacrifices himself to rescue Hiro and the missing daughter, and the professor is brought to justice and his plans foiled. Hiro rebuilds Baymax and the team goes on to help those in need.

Behind the Animation

- Baymax's movement was modeled after the movement of a baby with a full diaper. The inflatable, vinyl design is inspired by "soft robotics" research at Carnegie Mellon University.

- Although loosely based on a Marvel comic book, the film does not share the same universe as the live-action Marvel Cinematic Universe of films. Marvel legend Stan Lee voices Fred's father.

- The "Port of San Fransokyo" scene has over 6,000 people in it. There were 23 districts built in 3D, and 83,149 lots of the 150,000 in all of San Francisco were also built, along with 18.8 million building parts, 215,000 streetlights, 260,000 trees, and over 200 distinct advertising signs.

- Story artist Kendelle Hoyer felt that Hiro's family needed a pet. So, even though it wasn't in the script, she kept drawing a cat in all of her storyboards and eventually it became a part of the film. In the film, there is a picture hanging in the stairway of Hiro's house with Mochi the cat wearing a Stitch costume.

- The model of the design of Baymax's face is a Japanese traditional bell, called *Suzu*. Director Don Hall says that he got an inspiration when he visited a temple in Japan.

Quotable Quotes

It is alright to cry. Crying is a natural response to pain.

— Baymax

This is not my real face and body.

— Fred

Those who suffer a loss require contact from friends and/or loved ones.

— Baymax

I believe the world can be made into a happier, and much brighter, place, through the thorough application of nature's toolbox—chemistry!

— Honey Lemon

About the Author

Jim Korkis is an internationally respected Disney historian whose hundreds of articles and presentations about all things Disney have been enjoyed by people worldwide for decades.

He is the author of several popular Disney related books including *The Vault of Walt* series, *Who's Afraid of the Song of the South?*, *The Book of Mouse*, and *Who's the Leader of the Club? Walt Disney's Leadership Lessons*.

He feels he has become a better person by trying to heed the words of Jiminy Cricket even if he sometimes still gets led astray to Pleasure Island and makes a donkey of himself on occasion.

More Books from Theme Park Press

Theme Park Press publishes dozens of books each year for Disney fans and for general and academic audiences. Here are just a few of our titles. For the complete catalog, including book descriptions and excerpts, please visit:

ThemeParkPress.com

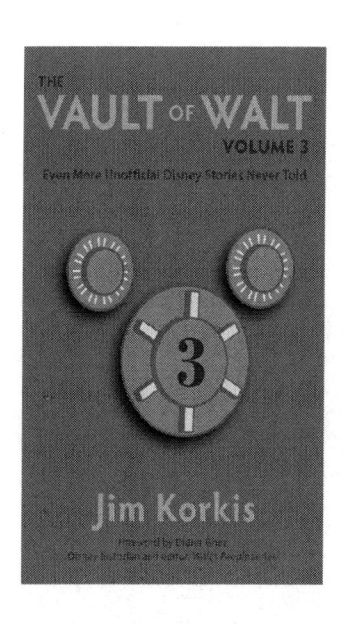

It's A Crazy Business: The Goofy Life of a Disney Legend
Pinto Colvig
Edited and Introduced by Todd James Pierce

Mouse In Transition: An Insider's Look at Disney Feature Animation
Steve Hulett
Foreword by John Musker, Disney Feature Films Animation Director

A Historical Tour of Walt Disney World, Volume 1
Andrew Kiste

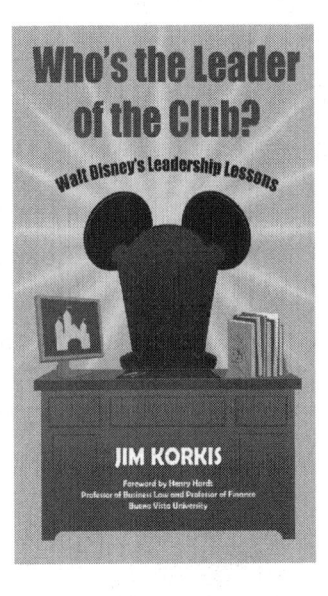

Who's the Leader of the Club? Walt Disney's Leadership Lessons
Jim Korkis
Foreword by Henry Hordt, Professor of Business Law and Professor of Finance, Buena Vista University

Great Big Beautiful Tomorrow

Walt Disney and Technology

Christian Moran
with Rolly Crump,
Bob Gurr, Jim Korkis,
Sam Gennawey and Dr.
Maureen Furniss, PhD

"Prepare to be enchanted, bewildered and mesmerized by this beat-by-beat account of the Haunted Mansion's creation." — Guillermo del Toro, Award-winning film director

The Unauthorized Story of Walt Disney's Haunted Mansion

Jeff Baham

Foreword by Rolly Crump

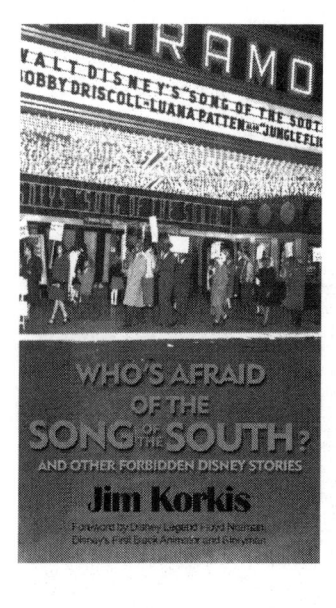

WALT DISNEY'S SONG OF THE SOUTH
BOBBY DRISCOLL · LUANA PATTEN in "JUNGLE FLI..."

WHO'S AFRAID OF THE SONG OF THE SOUTH?

AND OTHER FORBIDDEN DISNEY STORIES

Jim Korkis

Foreword by Disney Legend Floyd Norman,
Disney's First Black Animator and Storyteller

Walt Disney AND THE PROMISE OF Progress City

SAM GENNAWEY

Foreword by Werner Weiss

From Jungle Cruise Skipper to Disney Legend
40 Years of Magical Memories at Disney
William "Sully" Sullivan

Disneyland Secrets
GAVIN DOYLE

The Ride Delegate
Memoir of a Walt Disney World VIP Tour Guide
Annie Salisbury

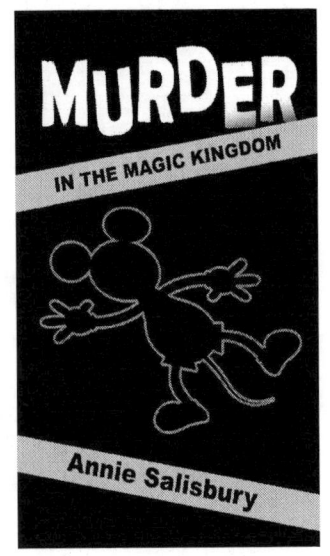

Murder in the Magic Kingdom
Annie Salisbury

Made in the USA
Lexington, KY
30 July 2015